MW01629202

Bow Down to
WILLINGHAM

Bow Down to WILLINGHAM

How White Guilt Enabled a Secretly Malicious Coach to Destroy the Once-Mighty Washington Huskies

by

Derek Johnson

PREVIOUS BOOKS BY DEREK JOHNSON

Husky Football in the Don James Era
and
The Dawgs of War: a Remembrance

Bow Down to Willinghan

Derek Johnson Books, LLC
www.DerekJohnsonBooks.com

ISBN: 978-0-9793271-3-1

Editor: Lucy Chen
Cover Design: Jane Sheppard
Book Layout: Jonathan Gullery
All photos by Kim Grinolds except as noted

Printed in the United States of America

Contents

Prologue 7
Chapter 1: The Coon Chicken Inn 15
Chapter 2: Willingham Comes To Washington 25
Chapter 3: Cleaning Up the Program 41
Chapter 4: The Willingham Way 45
Chapter 5: A Visit with Jamal Fountaine 53
Chapter 6: A Visit with Caesar Rayford 59
Chapter 7: The Lazy Recruiter 65
Chapter 8: A Visit with Craig Chambers 71
Chapter 9: A Visit with C. J. Wallace 79
Chapter 10: A Visit with Isaiah Stanback 93
Chapter 11: White Was Seeing Red 101
Chapter 12 : Suddenly Senior 109
Chapter 13: A Visit with Michael Braunstein 123
Chapter 14: Birth of the Mora Revolution 129
Chapter 15: Enter the Savior 135
Chapter 16: The Miseducation of Jake Locker 151
Chapter 17: Regional Civil War 159
Chapter 18: Emmert's Hour of Decision 169
Chapter 19: Mitchie the Kid's Rant 177
Chapter 20: Emmert Reflects 183
Chapter 21: Apocalypse 189
Chapter 22: A Visit with Mike Gastineau 207
Chapter 23: Woodward Reflects 213
Chapter 24: Sark Comes to Washington 219
Chapter 25: A Visit with "Angry Alum" 223
Epilogue 231
Acknowledgements 237

Touchdown Jesus looking over Notre Dame Stadium.

Tyrone Willingham's Fighting Irish prepare to take the field

Prologue

"I'm sure everybody ever associated with Notre Dame will tell you color had nothing to do with letting Willingham go, that it's totally a coincidence, which is like spitting in somebody's face and telling him it's a rain drop."

—Michael Wilbon, columnist,
Washington Post, December 2004

FIRINGS are messy and never fun, especially when they happen to good people. Tyrone Willingham, former *Sporting News* Coach of the Year, took a seat at a table in the Joyce Center Football Auditorium. His ever-stoic eyes gazed upon the reporters, who gathered to receive more information on the breaking news: Notre Dame had fired Willingham, the first black head football coach in its glamorous, Irish-Catholic dominant history, after only three years.

Willingham's firing ignited an emotional firestorm that was searing its way across the nation's airwaves, newspapers and the internet. Reverend Jesse Jackson castigated Notre Dame for lacking integrity. Richard Lapchick, of the Institute for Diversity and Ethics in Sports at the University of Central Florida, called Willingham the most significant hire in the history of college football and expressed deep concern. At the same time, forty protestors picketed the Notre Dame Campus, carrying signs reading: "$ COST NOTRE DAME ITS INTEGRITY", "WE WANT TY BACK", and "NEVER BEFORE - NEVER AGAIN". Chandra Johnson, an African-American assistant to outgoing President Reverend Malloy, shaved her head in protest of the firing. She said it would remain that way until Notre Dame won a national championship, since it seemed that was all the university cared for anymore. And Malloy himself spoke out in outrage, making it clear he completely opposed the firing. "The philosophical shift we have taken is a significant one," he said. "I am not happy about it, and I do not take responsibility for it."

Facing the reporters, Willingham took responsibility. "To say I am disappointed very much misses the mark," he said. "But at the same time, I understand that I did not meet the expectations or standards I set for myself. When you don't meet the expectations of yourself, you leave yourself vulnerable to the will of others. So today, I am no longer the head football coach at Notre Dame."

Notre Dame athletic director Kevin White explained the university's rationale: "From Sunday through Friday our football program has exceeded all expectations in every way. Tyrone has done some wonderful things, but again on Saturday, we've struggled. We've been up and down and sideways, a little bit inconsistent. I think the program is closer than when he arrived. I think we are making progress, but in my view and in the view of the university, we just didn't make enough progress. All of us had great expectations when we sat here three years ago, and in a number of ways, Tyrone has been an excellent fit and a great representative of the program. He personally has displayed impeccable integrity and tremendous character, and his players have represented themselves off the field in a first-class manner. In addition, our football program under his watch has never been stronger in terms of its academic performance."

Senior associate athletic director John Heisler announced Willingham would take one more question. A reporter started talking, but Willingham cut him off. "No, that was the last one. Thank you. My wish will be that this program will have great success in the future, and that whoever the coach is, I hope he comes in and does a great job because I believe there are some great young men in this program."

A moment later Willingham was gone, from both the press conference and Notre Dame.

Notre Dame's reputation was under siege from all corners. Columnist David Steele of the Baltimore Sun called for a discrimination lawsuit against Notre Dame. ESPN.com writer Alan Grant, the author of a book about Willingham's debut season, predicted that Notre Dame would now lower their standards and allow recruits of suspect character onto campus, all in the name of winning.

Michael Wilbon, a columnist with *The Washington Post,* pulled no punches. "People at institutions such as Notre Dame don't sit around anymore, even off the record, talking about getting rid of a person because he's a certain color. Such a conversation, if proven, would be illegal in this country, and most folks aren't that dumb. Intolerance has increasing subtlety. But the passionate distaste for Willingham in some quarters, including on campus after a loss, had an unmistakable stink to it."

What stunk for so many people was an unwritten but adhered-to rule that Notre Dame coaches always received a minimum of five years to establish their programs. Willingham had been hired to restore the luster to Notre Dame's legacy, dulled in recent years by mediocrity. Over the course of his three seasons in South Bend, Willingham's Fighting Irish went 21-15 and two of those teams went to bowl games.

But several embarrassing blowout losses and deep concerns over recruiting stoked anger and worry from many fans. The board of trustees fretted too. Following the season-ending 41-10 loss to #1 USC, the board held an all-night meeting to discuss Willingham's future. Then chairman Patrick McCartan and trustee Phillip Purcell spearheaded the firing without Father Malloy's approval and without having gone through the school's faculty board. Something behind the scenes prompted the board of trustees to take that drastic action. In doing so, they knew they were kicking a monumental hornet's nest.

Those that spoke to Willingham right after the firing reported him as being edgy and frustrated. He may have been down, but he wasn't without options. Unbeknownst to the media, he was mulling overtures from Seattle to become the next head football coach of the University of Washington Huskies.

Soon after the press conference, recruiting analyst Tom Lemming arrived on the Notre Dame campus and encountered a stunned Willingham. In a rare display of vulnerability, Willingham let down his guard.

"Tyrone asked me what went wrong for him there," Lemming recalled. "I told him that he needed a staff that would go after the great players. His staff really let him down. Tyrone was an honest recruiter and a good person. But he never attracted the great black athletes. That probably hurt him the most. Notre Dame has always been able to attract the great white athletes. The thinking was Tyrone would be able to attract the great black athletes. The thought was that that combination would have made Notre Dame unbeatable."

Recognized as the nation's leading expert on college football recruiting, Lemming is part of the CBS College Sports Network. He logs approximately 55,000 miles each year visiting the top recruits in the country. He's also the editor of Prep Football Report, considered to be the "Bible of the football recruiting industry," and he annually selects the team for the U.S. Army All-American Bowl. Michael Lewis, author of *The Blind Side: Evolution of a Game*, recognized Lemming as the "only national football scout in America."

"Willingham had one great recruiting class in 2002 and then two really bad ones after that," Lemming said. "In my opinion, Tyrone Willingham is an excellent coach and a perfect fit for Notre Dame, and his only mistake was not having a staff that knew how to sign great players. It's not my opinion, its fact that when you look at his last two recruiting classes at Notre Dame, they were arguably the two worst in Notre Dame history. Only one player got drafted. That's the worst in Notre Dame history in regards to the NFL draft. While the head coaches get the final blame, 90% of the work is done by the assistant coaches. They really let him down. He was too loyal to them."

Lemming found Willingham to be as pleasant as any other coach. "He's a great guy, a nice guy, and maybe one of the most honest coaches I've ever run into," Lemming said. "I've been in this business 32 years. Honesty and being a great recruiter don't go hand in hand. The more honest you are, the less likely you are to get a great player. Tyrone was honest to a fault; he looked you in the eye. I didn't know him well, like I know Urban Meyer or Kirk Ferentz, but I liked the guy a lot."

Notre Dame, with its seven Heisman Trophy winners and eight national championships, boasted a tradition without equal across the country. Being the only team in college football with its own television contract with NBC Sports enabled devoted alumni from coast to coast to catch every game. And for the fanatical fans that followed recruiting, Willingham's results brought them to panic.

"Instead of battling USC, Florida and USC, they were battling the Dukes, Northwesterns and Stanfords," Lemming said. "That's okay if you're Stanford, but if you're Notre Dame that's going to draw the ire of the fans. Notre Dame is the most talked-about program in the country, and has the most pushy and obnoxious fans who will get on your back no matter what you do. Stanford has the highest academic standards of all the big time schools, so they always had to go after a different type of ballplayer. That was the perfect place for Tyrone. He understood Stanford recruiting and I thought he did a real good job there.

"But the situation at Notre Dame is a bit of hypocrisy. Their academic standards are high but not any higher than Northwestern or others schools, and certainly lower than Stanford. They can let in kids that are borderline students. Everything there is arbitrary. That's why Notre Dame people hate me here in Chicago, because they try to come out as if they're a great academic institution. The fact is of the top 100 [recruits], Notre Dame could get 75 into school while Stanford could get maybe 5. Other schools could get all 100. In my opinion, it's easier to recruit to Notre Dame than many other schools, you just have to have the work ethic that has brought elite players there for the 100 years of football at the school. Notre Dame is obviously an elite school. It's my philosophy that when you're one of the sixteen elite schools, recruiting is different. Stanford isn't one of them obviously, but Notre Dame is. That means you have to recruit against the great teams to get the great players. And I've talked to Nick Saban, Pete Carroll, Mack Brown and Urban Meyer about it. And all of them say that no matter how good of a coach you are, you have to recruit the impact players, the difference makers. That's how you remain a consistently great team, and that's how those teams are always there. Not because they're better coaches, but because they're better recruiters."

At the end of the day, for whatever the reason, Willingham couldn't recruit. That fact, according to Lemming, sealed his fate at South Bend.

"If Tyrone Willingham had a staff that knew how to recruit impact players, he would still be at Notre Dame," he said. "It's that simple. He was a good coach and was just what Notre Dame was looking for in terms of integrity and honesty. All the integrity and honesty in the world won't do you any good if you don't win games. Notre Dame was a bit hypocritical in that regard. By the end of the 2004 season, they were getting bombed on the field by Southern Cal and had no top recruits in sight. I think the Notre Dame administration panicked and fired him."

W

Coon Chicken Inn logo.

Union protest of Coon Chicken Inn, circa 1940 (photos courtesy of Scott Farrar)

CHAPTER 1

The Coon Chicken Inn

"All progress is precarious, and the solution of one problem brings us face to face with another problem."

—Martin Luther King, Jr.

IN the depression-era Seattle of the 1930s, one could escape the city limits by heading north and crossing 85th into what is today the Lake City neighborhood. From there, people could enter the Coon Chicken Inn restaurant through the caricature of a giant, smiling Negro's face. The door swung open through the middle of the mouth, as one of the eyes perpetually winked and a porter's cap sat atop his head. Families passing through the entry could sit down inside and enjoy Fried Coon Chicken sandwiches, hamburgers and chicken pie while an orchestra and cabaret performed.

The giant Negro face served as a roadside attraction along that gaudy stretch of the old Bothell Highway. Roadhouses and whorehouses flanked both sides of the thoroughfare. Maxon Lester Graham, owner of the Coon Chicken Inn, used the Negro face as a logo, placing it on every dish, silverware item, menu, and paper product. Many whites regarded it as exotic kitsch.

Graham often hired black waiters and waitresses, and white kids dining at the restaurant looked at them with fascination. At the time, Seattle's black population was a mere 3,000. Many black citizens felt denigrated by the restaurant, but protests exacted little change. The fact that a full page ad ran in *The Seattle Times* advertising the restaurant speaks to the mindset of the Depression era. Simply put, the

Coon Chicken Inn served as a distillation of greater Seattle's racial worldview: blacks were a caricatured novelty.

At the University of Washington, the mindset permeated the football program. As of 1935, only two blacks had ever played for the Husky football team. Graduating from Seattle's Garfield High School that year was Charley Russell, a fleet-footed and heralded running back. At Garfield, he had earned ten letters, including three in football and three more in basketball. James Phelan, Washington's football coach, made no contact with Russell and indicated no interest. Washington State, Oregon and UCLA all expressed interest in Russell, but his mother refused to allow him to leave the Seattle area.

Left with no other choice, Russell walked on at Washington in the fall of 1936. Phelan subsequently offered him a scholarship, but Russell didn't play enough to letter. The Huskies ended the season with a loss to Pittsburgh in the Rose Bowl.

With the 1937 season about to begin, the *Seattle PI* piqued the public's interest with this tantalizing report: "When Charley Russell gets in the game, which Phelan says he will, you will see a dashing, young ball carrier… who runs as if his feet are on fire." But it soon became clear Russell would not factor prominently in Washington's plans. For some games during his sophomore season, he never left the bench. In others, he carried the ball only once or twice. In one game against Stanford, Russell carried the ball repeatedly as the Huskies mounted a drive. When Washington approached the 20-yard line, Phelan pulled Russell from the game. The drive stalled, and Stanford prevailed 13-7. In the aftermath, the *Seattle PI* summed up Russell's electrifying performance: "Charley Russell, the twisting, squirming, hot-footed Negro boy from Garfield! What a grand game he played and what an ovation he received as, tired and weary, he finally dragged his bruised body from the battle scene."

Russell barely played the rest of the season. The following fall, prior to what would have been his junior year, Russell went into Phelan's office to complain. "It told him I wasn't getting enough playing time," Russell later recalled. "Phelan told me I was lucky to have a scholarship, that many white boys would like to have the scholarship. That ended it. I quit the team, went to California and never played football again. I honestly feel he was a very prejudiced man and nobody will convince me otherwise... Guess I was born twenty years too soon. I just wanted to play football."

The next two decades showed steady increases in the number of black football players at Washington, though they were still greatly outnumbered by whites. Times were changing as the civil rights movement and its primary leader, Dr. Martin Luther King, rose to prominence. From 1957 onward, King served as president for the Southern Christian Leadership Conference, in the effort to provide leadership for the burgeoning movement. King drew upon Christianity for the ideals and studied Gandhi for operational techniques. Over the course of his career, Dr. King would travel over six million miles and speak over 2,500 times, including once at the University of Washington in November 1961 to a packed auditorium at the old Meany Hall. Following a thunderous standing ovation, King gave his speech on segregation and civil liberties.

He made a handful of speeches during that Seattle visit, and saw controversy erupt when First Presbyterian Church withdrew its offer to let him speak at their facility. Nevertheless, his trip was productive. After his final lecture, he asked longtime friend Reverend Samuel McKinney to take him to a barbecue restaurant in Seattle's Central Area. As McKinney later recalled, they spent several hours discussing issues and reminiscing about their college days. King said he was impressed by the progressive attitude he saw in the city.

Come 1967, racial unrest was tearing the country apart. Civil rights activist Stokely Carmichael spoke at the University of Washington and Garfield High School; it was here that he coined the term "Black Power." In these speeches, Carmichael emphasized that freedom cannot be given, only denied. The activist's job is not to demand that blacks be given freedom, but rather to civilize and separate America from its racism.

"If you take that to its logical conclusion," said Carmichael, "you would say that any civil rights bill that was passed in this country might have eased the struggle for black people but helped civilize white America. Let me give you an example. I'm black. I know that I'm black. I know that I'm a human being. And I know with that comes certain dignities that all human beings have. One of those is that I'm able to enter a public place. But now there are some dumb honkies who don't know that. So that every time I try to enter a store, the honky gets in my way, shoots at me, bombs my church, kills my children, or beats me up. 'Cause he doesn't know that I'm a human being. So the white folk in Washington, DC got to write a Civil Rights Bill to tell this honky, 'When I come, get out my way. . .get out my way. . . get out my way.' So that what they've done is they've civilized this honky—because I'm the same man I was, I'm just going to the store. The only trouble is that he is now forced to recognize my humanity. That's very important. And the same thing is true about the Voting Rights Act. We're black, we know we should be able to vote, every time we try to vote some honky stops us. So they got to pass a civil rights bill to stop him from denying us our rights. They don't give us anything! You've got to get that clear in your mind… They have bombed our churches, they have shot us in the streets, they have lynched us, they have cattle-prodded us, they have thrown lye over us, they have dragged our children out in the night. We have been the recipients of violence for over 400 years."

That more aggressive mindset impacted Husky football the following year. In 1968, *Life Magazine* published an article identifying thirteen UW football players who believed themselves to be victims of discrimination by Husky coaches and the athletic department. They issued four demands:

(1) Neutralization of head coach Jim Owens' powers through formation of a four-man black athletic committee which would be consulted on such matters as demoting a black player to the second string;
(2) A review of all coaches to bring to light examples of prejudice and discriminatory practices;
(3) Immediate dismissal of Bob Peterson, trainer, because of his alleged inferior, perfunctory treatment of injuries, and his reported use of the word "nigger"; and
(4) Permanent appointment of a black coach or administrator to bridge the gap in communications between the black athlete and the administration.

Owens met with the black players and agreed to two of the four demands. Peterson was fired, and Carver Gayton, a black who played fullback on Washington's 1960 Rose Bowl team, was hired as an assistant coach and intermediary.

Throughout the United States —especially on college campuses— racial tensions smoldered and flared. The "black power" movement emerged as a political force fueled by the assassination of Martin Luther King, Jr. And Washington football, slogging through a horrible season on the field, began to unravel off it. The demotion of black fullback Landy Harrell, set into motion four dramatic days. Black players, furious at what they perceived to be a demotion backed by racism, held a meeting with Gayton. They spoke of potentially boycotting the upcoming UCLA game in Los Angeles.

Gayton reported the players' new concerns to Owens, who immediately organized a team meeting before practice. Wanting to resolve the situation and restore team unity, he asked anyone with grievances to stay behind while the rest of the team took to the field. However, not a single person remained. Feeling frustrated, he addressed the team again out on the practice field and called for every player to pledge 100% loyalty. Four black players would not give that pledge, and Owens suspended them from the team.

This set off an outburst of controversy which led several hundred black and sympathetic white protestors to surround the Husky team bus so it couldn't depart for Sea-Tac Airport. The mob refused to disperse until the remaining eight black players disembarked and stayed behind. They did so, and the white players continued on their way to Los Angeles, where they would fall to the Bruins 61-20.

Georg Myers, sports editor of *The Seattle Times*, unloaded on Owens in his November 2, 1969 column. He claimed that the loyalty oath "reflected almost a suicidal impulse... It is not inconceivable that some players with reservations as to Owens and his program felt constrained to pledge 100 per cent. There is no evidence that Owens said that anyone who faltered in the pledge would be sacked... Owens suspended the four, and all were black. It was not surprising that black discrimination became the outcry."

The following Saturday, Washington hosted Stanford at Husky Stadium. Thunderous applause greeted Owens and the team, which was bizarre for a 0-7 football squad. The next day, citing misunderstandings on both sides, Owens reinstated the four black players.

For Husky football, and by extension the city of Seattle, tensions and misunderstandings remained on high for another couple years. Two key hirings of blacks by the UW athletic department would help to restore peace. Ray Jackson, a star Husky linebacker in the early sixties, was hired as an assistant coach. And Donald K. Smith, a former Seattle sportswriter and public relations worker for AT&T in New York, was hired as associate athletic director. In time, the black community came to feel heard and respected thanks to the work of Smith. The Black Athletes Alumni Club, which once threatened to discourage black athletes from attending Washington, reversed its position.

By the 1975 season, Owens was gone and Don James was in his debut season with the Huskies. Playing quarterback for Washington was Warren Moon—the first black quarterback in Husky history. Moon's promotion to first string over the incumbent starter Chris Rowland caused rancor among many fans. Over James' first two seasons, the Huskies went 6-5 and 5-6. The 1977 season started 1-3, including losses to lowly Syracuse and Minnesota. Seattleites picked up their torches and pitchforks, with their wrath concentrated upon James and Moon.

As Don James wrote in his 1990 autobiography *James*: "We try to look at right guard the same as left guard. And right tackle the same as quarterback. It's just two guys competing for a job. You let them compete and then—regardless of how they have played in the past—you start the one who is doing the best job at the moment… Some people tried to make it a black-white issue. Some would have you believe that Moon was booed because he was black. What was happening, the thing we tried to emphasize to Warren was that if you're a quarterback, it doesn't matter what color you are. If you don't move the ball and don't win, you're going to get booed. But we stuck with him."

That dedication came to fruition as that '77 season progressed. A 54-0 win over Oregon began a new era in Washington football. In mid-November, Washington battled powerhouse USC in Husky Stadium with the Rose Bowl berth on the line. Washington led 21-10 in the fourth quarter, when Moon dropped back to pass. Not seeing anyone open, he took off—and raced 71 yards for a touchdown. The crowd went nuts. For a moment James thought he heard more booing, but then realized fans had changed "BOO" to "MOON". Six weeks later, Moon would be named MVP of the Rose Bowl as the Huskies beat Michigan 27-20.

As another two decades passed, societal evolution continued its march. Black Americans, and Americans in general, experienced the greatest economic prosperity in history. For blacks, part of that opportunity stemmed from the effects of affirmative action that used quotas in hiring practices. Heading toward a new millennium, the heated debate centered around fairness and the idea of a colorblind society. Come 1998, Washington voters passed Initiative 200 which effectively banned affirmative action on college campuses.

As Seattle ushered in the new millennium, the days of Charley Russell and the Coon Chicken Inn were long-forgotten relics. As for Husky football, head coaches Don James and Jim Lambright had each come and gone, and Rick Neuheisel now led the way. He was, in fact, the focal point of a story raising eyebrows across the country.

Neuheisel was hot on the recruiting trail after Kellen Winslow, Jr., a prep All-American receiver out of San Diego, and son of black NFL Hall-of-Famer Kellen Winslow, Sr. The youngster had narrowed his decision to three schools: Miami, Michigan State and Washington. A nationally televised press conference had been scheduled for weeks, and the college football world largely suspected that he would select Washington.

But the night before signing day, father and son continued a long, drawn-out argument that had raged privately for weeks. Given that Kellen was under the age of 21, a legal guardian had to sign his papers. The son had decided he wanted to go to Washington, but his father disagreed. "I know it's your decision," said Winslow, Sr. "You're still immature about this and you don't know what's going to happen at Washington. I don't trust them."

Come the day of the press conference, in a room adjacent to the TV cameras, Kellen clutched the unsigned letter-of-intent papers and waited anxiously to tell the world he was headed to Washington. But there was still no agreement, and Winslow, Sr. announced his family needed more time to decide.

Quoted later by Wayne Drehs of ESPN.com, the son described the drama: "We went at it. I was begging him to sign the papers because I really wanted to go to Washington. But it didn't work out. We had to postpone everything because we couldn't agree."

Finally, the announcement was made, and football fans from Coral Gables, Florida cheered with jubilation. Kellen Winslow, Jr. was headed to Miami. A deciding factor, it turned out, boiled down to Winslow, Sr. feeling Washington's coaching staff was being a little too slick in their recruiting practices. But the fact Neuheisel was white didn't help matters. Winslow, Sr. expressed enthusiasm toward institutions headed by black coaches.

"I don't care what people say, race is still an issue in this country," Winslow, Sr. said on the air. "Those who say it isn't have their heads buried. They live in another country… I have no qualms telling you that if I were being recruited right now, I'd go to Michigan State or Stanford." At that time, Michigan State was led by head coach Bobby Williams and Stanford by Tyrone Willingham—both black.

Interestingly enough, Miami's coach at that time was Butch Davis, a white man, and Miami had three black assistant coaches to Washington's two. The national media's consensus was that Miami was a choice born of compromise. Whether this really was the case isn't clear, although Winslow, Sr. did state that he preferred his son go to Michigan State. What was crystal clear was that the father had prevented the son from going to Washington. His comments created a national uproar within the college football world. Despite possible hypocrisies, part of his argument did stand on solid footing. For all the life-affirming opportunities that blacks had gained, the number of head coaching opportunities for them in college football remained severely limited.

That was certainly a concern held by Todd Turner as he became athletic director at the University of Washington in 2004. As Husky football slogged through its first losing season in 27 years, Turner initiated contact with Notre Dame's Tyrone Willingham in mid-season.

Turner desperately wanted him to be the Husky coach, and in time he would land him. Three years later, Turner would fire his women's basketball coach June Daugherty, despite having just gone to the NCAA tournament, to hire first-time head coach Tia Jackson to lead the way. Counting Lorenzo Romar, head coach of the men's basketball team, Washington's three most visible sports programs had African-Americans leading the way. Turner couldn't have been prouder. He beamed whenever the topic was broached by others.

Turner assumed everyone would be swayed and deeply moved by the historical precedence, but he didn't know or understand football players. One prominent Husky player from the Willingham era could only shake his head as he recalled that time. "The administration was so proud that they had a black football coach and two black basketball coaches," he said. "Who gives a shit? Players don't care if they're playing for a black coach, white coach, green coach, or whatever. Guys want someone who will help them win games and get to the NFL."

Tyrone Willingham at his first fall camp as Washington coach

CHAPTER 2

Willingham Comes To Washington

"I hope anything I do in my life will be very positive, because I'd like for my kids to look at their father and say he had a life that was very positive and he fulfilled his dreams and the dreams of others."

—Tyrone Willingham, 2002

SOARING high above glittering Lake Washington, a seaplane began its descent. On board was Washington football coach Rick Neuheisel, along with his most highly-prized recruit, Reggie Williams. The rest of the Pac-10 knew that if Neuheisel could land Williams, rated by Prep Football Report as the nation's #1 receiver, defensive backs throughout the conference could plan on being scorched for long touchdowns for the foreseeable future. Neuheisel, fresh off winning the Rose Bowl with an 11-1 record, was pulling out all the stops. He was amassing a respected recruiting class and Williams would be the crown jewel. A joyous Neuheisel later boasted with mock humility: "I called him every day it was legal to do so, and the neat thing was he never seemed tired of talking to me."

Minutes later the plane made a smooth splash landing and pulled alongside the dock of Neuheisel's lakeside home. Waiting for them was the coach's wife Susan with a gigantic smile on her face and a plate of fresh-baked cookies in her hands. The famous Neuheisel charm was kicking into overdrive, closing in on another recruiting kill.

The 39-year old coach had already snared a verbal commitment from a big-time quarterback out of New Lenox, Illinois named Casey Paus. Sitting in his bedroom, Paus received a call from Neuheisel one evening, asking him to talk to Williams and encourage him to be a

Husky. Casey gladly dialed the number. When Williams picked up, Paus talked football with him, envisioning what it would be like for them to be a dynamic duo in the years to come. With the enthusiasm of an overexcited puppy, Paus blurted out, "I heard your school has field turf. That's so cool!" Years later Paus looked back on that phone call with a shake of the head. "He must have been thinking, who's this goofball from the Midwest?"

But a few weeks later, Williams electrified the Seattle area with his announcement that he was picking the Huskies. And Paus was coming too. In Casey, the Huskies were getting the Gatorade Illinois State Player of the Year. As a four-year starter for Lincoln Way Central High School, Paus amassed a 42-2 record including a 12-1 mark his senior year, leading the Knights to #3 in the state. The accolades poured in as The Sporting News, PrepStar and SuperPrep anointed him All-American. Rivals.com listed him as the sixth-best quarterback in America. To top it off, he carried a 4.0 GPA. He would be playing in the same conference as his brother Corey, who was heading into his senior season as UCLA's starting quarterback.

As Rose Bowl MVP Marques Tuiasosopo moved on to the NFL, Paus became the backup to quarterback Cody Pickett. Over the next two season Paus witnessed events no one could have foreseen: the erosion of Washington's powerful running game and the firing of Rick Neuheisel in June 2003 for lying to NCAA investigators about his participation in a neighborhood gambling pool on basketball games. Offensive Coordinator Keith Gilbertson took over as the head coach and braced himself as best he could.

On a crisp, cool October evening in 2003, everything was right in the world of Husky Football. The Oregon Ducks were in town for a night game at Husky Stadium that would be televised up and down the west coast. The high-flying Ducks bounded to a 10-0 lead and knocked Pickett out of the game in the second quarter. Now a third-year sophomore, Paus was suddenly under center. In one moment of magic, Paus broke huddle and came to the line of scrimmage at Washington's 37-yard line. Lining up wide left was Reggie Williams—and Paus noticed he was uncovered. Casey called an audible, but Reggie ignored it and ran his route. Paus didn't much care as the

Ducks had screwed up the coverage and all he had to do was deliver the ball cleanly to his target. He did so, hitting Williams in stride right at the midfield "W". Reggie sprinted past Oregon defenders all the way to the end zone. As Paus ran downfield to celebrate, he was acutely aware of the piercing air siren going off and the frantic roar of 70,000 purple-clad supporters. Paus pumped his fist and thought to himself, "this is the coolest fucking thing in the world!"

By the end of the night, Paus was the toast of Seattle. Filling in for Pickett, he completed 5 of 8 passes for 117 yards and 2 touchdowns. Washington destroyed Oregon 42-10. Players were happy. Fans were delirious. For the moment, all was well in Husky Nation.

But things weren't well for the Husky program overall. Earlier in the season, Nevada had dealt the Huskies a stunning defeat. A 54-7 loss in Berkeley to the California Bears left Washington with a 5-6 record. The Bears rolled through the Husky defense with startling ease, amassing an incomprehensible 720 yards of total offense. The following week, it took a dramatic 27-19 win over a top-5 Washington State Cougar team to avoid a losing season and conclude at 6-6.

Finishing the 2003 season with a .500 record was very important to everyone in the program. Washington had not experienced a losing season since 1976. By reaching 6-6, Washington continued its streak for the 27th consecutive year, second only to Nebraska. During that stretch, Washington had been to seven Rose Bowls and an Orange Bowl. It was a premiere program on the west coast. But dark clouds gathered on the horizon as the 2004 season approached.

With Pickett gone, Casey Paus assumed control on the offense. From the very first game against Fresno State, everything unraveled. The Bulldogs roughed up Washington in Seattle, which left Husky fans rubbing their eyes in disbelief. Paus was awful, completing just 18 of 39 passes for 183 yards and 3 interceptions. Casey's world had only begun to crumble. Washington would fall to 0-2 a week later, as UCLA tackled receiver Charles Frederick on their 1-yard line just as time expired. The Bruins escaped Seattle with a 37-31 win.

For the next game, Washington traveled to South Bend, Indiana to take on the most storied program in college football—the Notre Dame Fighting Irish. Storied as they may have been, the Irish were struggling to stay at .500 under coach Tyrone Willingham. For Paus, the day was a big one, because around forty family members and friends were making the trip from nearby Illinois to see him play.

"It was one of the hardest things I've ever had to deal with," Paus recalled. "One of the TV crews followed my parents around for the whole pregame and tailgate stuff and then followed them up into the stands. The game begins and we're losing, I'm not playing great but I've had worse days. Fans start talking shit about me and they're yelling at my parents. Gilbertson pulled me at halftime and Carl Bonnell played the second half and got a concussion. It was a breakdown point for me personally, and all I wanted to do was hug my mom."

Notre Dame went on to win 38-3, leaving the Huskies with an 0-3 record for the first time since 1969. Blaine Newnham of *The Seattle Times* wrote: "It is clear that Washington can't skip rope and chew gum at the same time." He then went on to quote Carl Bonnell who said: "I wanted to go to Washington to win. The Huskies have won forever. This is not where we're supposed to be. We're supposed to be playing to get to the Rose Bowl."

Several weeks later, there was no Rose Bowl, or winning season for that matter. After 27 consecutive years without a losing season, the Washington Huskies were completely derailing toward what would end up as a 1-10 record. The Seattle newspapers marveled at the historic level of futility. Speculation also abounded as to who would succeed outgoing coach Keith Gilbertson. The portly head coach was coming unhinged and completely powerless to stop the disastrous season from unraveling before him. On the practice field, Gilbertson and his staff constantly screamed as players beat each other to a pulp. For the players, encouragement was as rare as November sunshine in the Northwest. Off the field, Gilbertson sometimes sat in his office with lights dimmed or off, trying to calm his frayed nerves. As he would say later, "I have loved Husky football since I was a kid, and I will have to live with 1-10 for the rest of my life."

The latest twist now was that Washington's new athletic director, Todd Turner, was forming committees to build consensus for hiring the next football coach. He brought in a panel of players, including Casey Paus, defensive lineman Manase Hopoi, receiver Bobby Withorne, and linebacker Joe Lobendahn. As Turner addressed the players, he mentioned in turn the different coaches being considered. One player asked about California coach Jeff Tedford, but Turner quickly dismissed that as being impossible.

The players recalled Turner naming two possibilities: Tom O' Brien of Boston College and the recently-fired Tyrone Willingham of Notre Dame. Upon hearing Willingham's name, one of them voiced an objection. To everyone's surprise, Turner argued that Willingham would be a perfect fit for the University of Washington.

Both Paus and Hopoi left the meeting feeling like it had been just for show. Even still, Paus had heard that Willingham was a no-nonsense disciplinarian, and the idea of having that kind of coach excited him.

The moment of truth came soon after when Turner traveled to Chicago with UW president Mark Emmert to secretly interview Willingham. On the flight back to Seattle, Turner and Emmert intentionally didn't discuss who to offer the job to. They each wrote a name on a piece of paper and then revealed their selections: both men had written Tyrone Willingham. Upon returning home, Turner proudly got on the phone and offered Willingham the job. The Huskies had their new coach.

Paus and a couple of teammates were returning from a weekend trip to Canada when a radio report broke the news. The athletic department scheduled a team meeting for the next day. "I was pretty excited and anxious to meet him and see what he was all about," Paus recalled. "I was very optimistic, coming off that rather disappointing year. I was looking forward to starting with a fresh start."

A groundswell of excitement enveloped the University of Washington campus. Word quickly got around when Willingham was spotted at various places. The press conference of December 13, 2004 featured Willingham looking dapper in a suit and tie, with a whistle around his neck that he blew for effect.

Athletic director Todd Turner was first to speak, revealing that Willingham was the number one candidate all along, and that the position was never offered to anybody else. Willingham then pitched himself to the media.

"Tyrone Willingham is a great fit for the University of Washington," said Willingham. "It has been noted that he has integrity, is straightforward, intelligent, has the best interest of the players and university at heart, has been successful, developed young people, all that says he is a great fit for this university and I would hope a great fit at any university."

When a reporter asked about his thoughts on the Washington job, Willingham uttered words that quickly fired up a hungry fan base. "They know that when you say it is time for the University of Washington to return to being the Dawgs, and when you talk about the Dawgs in this program, that is a vicious animal."

The team room is located halfway up the famous Husky Stadium tunnel, with amphitheater-style seating positioned upon a gentle slope that gave view upon a podium. An excited buzz filled the air as Washington players filed into the room to meet their new coach. As Willingham and Turner stood off to the side chatting lightly, Casey Paus approached Willingham to welcome him to the program. Willingham nodded slightly but turned away and said nothing.

"I didn't think anything of it at the time," Paus said. "I was very excited. We will have a straight edge, disciplinary coach. And that felt like something we needed at that time. I've had always been a hard worker, to go out and bust my ass for that team. I thought my personality would fit in with his personality and work style."

As Willingham was officially introduced the room broke into thunderous applause. Guys were happy to see this famous face standing before them. Many of the black players felt a great swelling of pride and some had moist eyes.

"Willingham came in with his gray little suit on," said one of the black players who now plays in the NFL. "Everybody was pretty excited about it. Tyrone Willingham's name was everywhere. It was a prideful moment to be in the room and see the first black football coach in Washington history being introduced. We saw Willingham's face all over TV. It seemed like a cool deal. Then he opens his mouth. And the first thing he says is... 'Tyrone Willingham this, Tyrone Willingham that. And I guarantee that if you do things The Willingham Way, you will win.' Right then and there, we were like oh shit! Talking about himself in the third person, we were like who does this guy think he is? Nobody talks about themselves continuously unless you're Dwayne 'The Rock' Johnson, and that's for entertainment purposes only. Nobody does that shit, it was a clown move. It soured the moment."

At one point Willingham paused and asked if there were any questions. Casey Paus raised his hand. He explained that the two previous coaches, Rick Neuheisel and Keith Gilbertson were offensive-minded guys. What philosophy, asked Paus, did Willingham carry with him?

Willingham's eyes stared at the quarterback. "Coach Willingham coaches the coaches." Paus paused for a moment then asked what that meant. "It means that Coach Willingham picks the best coaches and then coaches them."

As Willingham resumed speaking for another hour, many players felt like he was trying to sell them that he deserved the job. He discussed growing up in Kinston, North Carolina and how his late mother Lilian taught elementary school for 38 years. He also went into detail regarding the experience of walking on at Michigan State in both football and baseball, and the coaching stops along the way including Stanford and the NFL's Minnesota Vikings. He began laying down new rules and preparing the players for what was to come.

"The first thing he wanted was us to be good students and good men," said defensive tackle Manase Hopoi. "He made it clear he wanted us to be great men before we became great players. A lot of us looked around and thought... Okay? Everybody there got recruited there to play football. Education is most important, but when you eat, sleep and drink football all day, that's all you think about. When someone comes in and says it's not important, it drains you. I didn't think of myself as a bad person or a non-professional person. So it was weird when he came in and says, 'Whoever you are now is not good enough. I'm going to make you better.' I was like, 'wow, okay. You mean I've been raised by my parents and coaches all this time to be the person I am, and then you're going to come in and tell me that I'm not a good enough person, especially when you don't even know me? This is how it's going to be? It was a condescending tone. I knew it was the beginning of a long season, a long struggle and a long fight against him to keep our traditions and identity alive."

That struggle began in January, following the holiday break. Willingham asked to be filled in as to the traditions and history that made Husky football unique. He soon received a report listing these out in detail. He began using that list as a reference guide to reshape the program. Players were no longer allowed to grow their hair out or have facial hair below the lip. There would be no swearing or spitting. Friendly hazing activities such as the "Moat Crawl" were all eliminated. In this long-standing activity, freshman players were blindfolded and forced to run 60 yards through the Husky Stadium moat, while upper classmen through water and Jello on them. The profane "Say Who" chant, which could be traced back to the Don James era and served as a beloved way for the team to rally, especially after wins, was banned. Black fraternity players were banned from doing their step shows, where they made rhythms with their hands and feet, and the freshmen would be coerced to perform in front of the whole team. Polynesian players could no longer have their singing and harmonizing group, where they would force freshmen to sing in front of the whole team.

"We'd say tell your little homie to do the step and tell us where he's from," said Manase Hopoi. "It built you stronger as a man, threaded out the weak-minded and brought the team together. Washington had its own secret traditions. They call it hazing and people think it's awful, but for us U-Dub athletes, it was more about toughness. To find that toughness in a new player to see how much they're going to fight in the battle. Just like when soldiers go through boot camp, and not everybody makes it through. Some give up, some quit. You don't want to go to war with somebody who is not going to fight to the death with you."

Even with such drastic changes, Casey Paus remained optimistic as spring practice for 2005 approached. He had high expectations for the team and relished the opportunity to put everything behind him. He would take the reigns and be an effective leader.

But he quickly discovered he'd been demoted from starter to

fourth string. In one of his few conversations with Willingham that spring, Willingham turned to him and said: "Do you know what your problem is Casey? You don't know how to deal with adversity."

When Paus heard that, with the tone of finality in which it was said, he knew it would be a long year. At the same time, however, time was running short for a Husky legend. Arguably the greatest Husky of all time, Steve Emtman had won the prestigious Outland Trophy and Lombardi Award in 1991 when the Huskies captured a share of the National Championship. After becoming the first player taken in the 1992 NFL Draft, Emtman played for seven disappointing seasons replete with injuries. Nonetheless, he left the game an extremely wealthy man. He returned to Washington in 2000 for just $30,000 a year to be the assistant strength coach to his former teammate Pete Kaligis.

In the first few months under Willingham, Emtman was offered the strength and conditioning job after Kaligis bolted for a coaching position with Division II Montana. But Emtman wasn't interested in overseeing the men's crew or women's softball teams. He simply wanted to oversee the football team. He even offered his own money to build a football-only weight room, but athletic director Todd Turner rejected the idea, saying it needed to be for all the student-athletes or none at all.

Push came to shove during the spring when Emtman became alarmed at the lack of organization he was witnessing. Emtman had played for Hall of Fame coaches Don James and Don Shula. He knew what a practice should look like. He took Willingham aside and asked what the overall plan was. Willingham gave an answer Emtman found indecipherable, so he asked again: "What is your plan Coach Willingham? I don't see any semblance of a plan here." According to Emtman, Willingham mumbled and talked in circles, never giving a clear answer.

That was that for Emtman. Willingham soon demoted him and then drummed him out of the program. To Husky players, it was the equivalent of seeing the Pope pushed down a flight of stairs.

By the end of spring practice for 2005, the drills felt disorganized to many players. They had stopped working on the little things that would help them improve. In past years, when special teams were being worked on, the defensive linemen would practice their hand placement, stance, and tackling. But instead of having those players working on their technique, Willingham would have the starters stand on the sideline and just watch, so they would understand what the special teams were trying to do. And players often stood motionless for twenty minutes at a time, practice after practice, not getting anything done.

By fall camp in August, Casey Paus spent most of his time on the field as the placeholder for extra points and field goals. Isaiah Stanback was the starter, followed by Oregon transfer Johnny DuRocher and Carl Bonnell. It hit Paus like a ton of bricks. He stood little chance of getting any playing time in the senior season that lay ahead. "Depression almost set in," he recalled. "It was like, 'am I going to get a shot here?' I was too naïve and too complacent that I got pushed aside. It's about the only regret I have that I didn't stand up for myself. At least to walk in there to Coach Willingham's office and ask, 'why?'"

Once the games began, things got ugly in a hurry. Willingham's Huskies collapsed in the opener against Air Force and would never recover. The following week, Jeff Tedford's Cal Bears walked into Husky Stadium and scored 56 points, the most ever surrendered to a Washington opponent at home since 1889. Notre Dame, Willingham's old team that was now led by coach Charlie Weis, came into Husky Stadium and ran roughshod 36-17. In consecutive games against Oregon, USC and Arizona State, the Huskies were outscored 140-65. Through it all, Casey Paus watched his senior season wither away to naught.

The season finale in late November saw Washington enter the Apple Cup with a 2-8 record. The game was at Husky Stadium. Although the Huskies led the Washington State Cougars 22-19 with 5:31 left in the game, the Cougars took over on their own 20-yard line. Eight plays later, it was second-and-nine from Washington's 39, when Cougar quarterback Alex Brink noticed that the Huskies were very slow in lining up. He quick-snapped the ball and threw a bubble screen pass to wide receiver Trandon Harvey, who zipped down the sideline for the winning touchdown with 1:20 left.

The scene at Husky stadium was surreal. 50,000 Husky fans sat stunned, while the remaining 20,000 Cougar fans dressed in crimson went bonkers. As the final seconds ticked off the clock, Hopoi looked across the field and saw the Cougars were about to storm the field and stomp on the large midfield W.

"I got to the W before they reached it," Hopoi said. "My right hand hooked and caught one player, and caught another. Willingham got in front of me and told me 'step back and walk away.' I moved Willingham out of the way and kept shoving people off the W. Once I got hit, it was over with. I started retaliating and throwing punches. My Polynesian connection were right behind me, and behind them were many of my other teammates. We were on the same page with that."

Things were volatile for a couple of minutes before officials and coaches separated the teams and herded them off the field. Nobody was injured. Years later, Hopoi still gets fired up remembering that day.

"Bleeding purple and gold for the five years at the U of W, seeing the type of great people we've had there, and the program, I wasn't going to let anyone disrespect our stadium, our field, our colors, our fans or alumni. And when I saw them heading to stomp on the W, that was the first thing that came to mind. I was like YOU GUYS AREN'T GOING TO CELEBRATE ON OUR W. YOU CAN MAYBE TRY IT NEXT TIME. BUT NOT THIS TIME, NOT WHILE I'M STILL HERE! That's how things were at Washington. That's how we were created. You're going to play, you're going to bleed, and you're going to die for that W. We had guys like Curtis Williams that played on that field and got paralyzed and died for that team. We've had other players who sacrificed so much to play for the fans, for alumni, and for the W. And so nobody was going to come and disrespect it. And for Coach Willingham to tell me to allow it, it was not happening. It just showed the lack of respect he had for the school and the W. He didn't care. I had family, friends and alumni who told me later that they appreciated me fighting for the W. And it felt good, to know that I wasn't by myself in doing that. Coach Willingham wasn't going to fight for us and for what we were about."

In the team room afterwards, Willingham's eyes flared with anger. He repeatedly stated that they had made him and the school look bad. He assured everyone in the room that he would be poring over the video to single out the main culprits and punish them. Later when Willingham addressed the media, he barely referenced the game or the defeat, choosing instead to focus on the fracas. He apologized to Washington State University and the fans that witnessed the altercation.

"He knew I led the charge," Hopoi said. "He was more worried about outside people's perceptions than his own players' perceptions. He tried some sort of punishment with me, but I never talked to him again after that game, never again associated with him. I was glad my career was over and that I would no longer be a part of a fake program."

Casey Paus was glad too. "There was a sense of relief that it was over," he said. "At the same time, there was anger, disappointment and hatred that it ended like that. Such a sour taste in my mouth and heart."

The 2005 season would officially conclude the following week at the annual team banquet at a downtown Seattle hotel. A video presentation was shown, featuring a handful of seniors speaking into the camera and expressing their memories and thoughts regarding their UW careers. When Casey Paus's turn came, he choked back tears as he apologized to his teammates. He had gone from starter to fourth string quarterback. He took the blame for the 2004 season. He told them that he loved every single one of them and never wanted to do anything but win football games.

Moments later, when offensive coordinator Tim Lappano was up on stage, he singled out Paus and expressed how much his work ethic and devotion to the team had meant to everybody. Every player rose to their feet to give Paus a prolonged standing ovation. "It didn't make everything worthwhile," sad Paus, "but at the same time I got part of my heart back and kind of got part of my swagger back."

"We're a family," Hopoi added. "As a family, not everything goes your way. I know that Casey Paus didn't want to throw that many interceptions that year and say that he was the reason for losing, but us as players, we know that happens and you can't change it. All you can do is better yourself and help your team in the years to come. Casey wasn't allowed that for his senior year in college. It was like he wasn't a part of the team at all. As soon as Willingham arrived, he never gave him a chance to compete and redeem himself. He didn't even give him a chance to talk and be a leader. When you see one of your brothers put down and you see one of your brothers work so hard for four years and then get pushed aside like a stepchild and not be seen at all, you're not going to look away and not see it. For us as a family, when he apologized, we knew what he was talking about. People all remember that season for the losses, but nobody will remember the hard things Casey did to help prepare us. And the leadership he showed off the field. He did a lot of things for guys on the team that had drinking problems or personal problems, he was always there for everybody. He was probably the smartest guy on the team. But like they say, tough times don't last, but tough people do. And there would be times where he wanted to leave that senior year. We were like 'Bro! You're going to leave the family? We're your family.' And he said 'I know… Geez, if it weren't for you guys I would be out of here.'"

With his collegiate playing days behind him, Paus received zero interest from agents and scouts. He continued working out in December, hopeful of some opportunity somewhere. And opportunity did knock, in the form of his brother Corey, the former UCLA and CFL quarterback. He had connections with a large agency in Los Angeles and the group organizing the Hula Bowl, the game in Hawaii that allowed seniors to showcase their talents for NFL scouts. As a favor to Corey, phone calls were made and the word that came back from the board was good: James Chow, a friend of Corey's, told Casey that if he paid his own way to Hawaii, it looked like they could make room for him as the third string quarterback on the West team.

In a twist of irony, the head coach of the western team was Tyrone Willingham.

Paus felt this was to his advantage. This was his one final shot. He called his girlfriend and told her the good news. It was an ecstatic moment for both of them. Then Casey called his brother. “He’s always been my go to guy,” Casey said. “For advice, confidence booster, troubles, brainstorming, you name it. He was excited and spent most of the time giving me a pep talk. I waited for dinner that night to enjoy a beer with my roommates. The game was only about ten days away.”

The next day, a jubilant Paus headed over to the UW football offices and knocked on Willingham’s office door. Willingham smiled and seemed happy to see him. Paus explained the situation and said it might take as long as Tuesday before things could be finalized.

“That’s great Casey,” said Willingham. “Don’t worry about Monday, that’s shorts and t-shirts, Tuesday we’ll be in shells. Wednesday will be the big day in full pads, so as long as you get there by then you will be okay.”

On Saturday, one week before the game, Paus called Chow. “Hang tight Casey, we’re still ironing out details. Have your bags packed.”

On Sunday, Casey called Chow again. Once again, he was told to hang tight but to be ready.

On Monday, Chow told Paus that the board had officially given approval for Paus to join the team. “They said you were good to go, but there’s a hang up. I don’t know what’s going on.”

On Tuesday, Chow told Paus: “We’re still looking good, should get you here tomorrow. Hang in there.”

Finally on Friday, the day before the game, Chow called Paus with the bad news. After the board had approved Paus, they had gone to Willingham and told him that Paus was going to be his third string quarterback. Willingham responded, “I don’t need him here, I have enough quarterbacks.”

And so Paus could only watch on TV as Auburn’s Tommy Tubberville lead the East to a 10-7 win over Willingam’s West squad.

The following week, when Willingham returned to Seattle, Paus requested a meeting with the UW coach. Then Paus walked into athletic director Todd Turner’s office and requested his presence at that meeting. “I told him that I wanted him to witness what his football coach had done.”

The meeting took place in Turner's office at the Graves Building, at a round table by the window. Willingham walked in and sat down.

"I want to talk to you about this whole Hula Bowl situation," said Paus. "I want to know why I wasn't allowed to go and participate."

"I felt that you were being promised something that you shouldn't have been promised," said Willingham. "I didn't think it was right."

"But I spoke to you a week before the game and you said congratulations. Didn't you say that?"

"Yes."

"So when you were over there, it didn't cross your mind to wonder where I was?"

"No."

"It didn't enter your mind, 'Hey, Casey played for me, he was coming over here, where is he?'"

"No," said Willingham with a cold stare.

"So let me get this straight. You could have reached out to help me get my last chance to ever get a shot, and it never occurred to you."

"No."

"So you had an opportunity to help me, but you chose not to."

"That's correct."

"So let me get this straight. After all you said in the media and to us players about wanting to help your players and help us with our futures, and you chose not to help me."

"Yes."

Paus looked over to Turner, who hadn't uttered a word. Turner just looked back at him blankly. Paus got up. "Well then thank you for your time," he said and exited the room.

Despite later claims that Rick Neuheisel left UW in shambles,
his team's 2003 graduation rate was 2nd in the Pac-10
and the police blotter was virtually clean

CHAPTER 3

Cleaning Up the Program

"A great deal of intelligence can be invested in ignorance when the need for illusion is deep."

—Saul Bellow, writer

WHEN Todd Turner became UW's athletic director on August 1, 2004, he inherited a program with 600 student-athletes and 23 sport programs. The most prominent program—football—hadn't had a losing season since 1976.

But the previous year had proved a difficult grind for the department. Barbara Hedges, the previous AD, had fired football coach Rick Neuheisel in June 2003 for participating in a high-stakes neighborhood betting pool for the NCAA basketball tournament, which was the focus of intense media and public scrutiny and sensationalizing. In truth, Neuheisel's primary faults were plummeting production in the running game, and too-slick recruiting practices that stretched rules and stirred resentment. His glib manner often rubbed people the wrong way. Perhaps that was why the media portrayed his involvement in the neighborhood gambling pool as something akin to a point shaving scandal.

Other stories also provided bad press to the UW. Softball players allegedly addicted to pain medications. Narcotic painkillers passed out freely to athletes in the athlete department, without exams or prescriptions. Members of the training staff getting into fights. 3,100 doses of various controlled substances issued in the name of one softball player in a two-year period. In the stretch of eleven months, 2,200 such doses were handed out to a UW trainer.

By the time Todd Turner arrived at UW, the university was awaiting word from a NCAA investigation regarding a potential lack of institutional control. It also had a pending court date with Neuheisel, who had filed a wrongful termination lawsuit. The protracted coverage of these events in the local media created a perpetual black cloud that hung over the program and created an implication of guilt. UW President Mark Emmert expressed happiness that Turner was on the job and appreciation for his reputation for integrity. "He emerged in the search process as the very best candidate," said Emmert, "and we're pleased he likes us as much as we like him."

By October 2004—Turner's third month on the job—the situation settled itself nicely. The NCAA imposed no penalties on Neuheisel for his participation in the neighborhood gambling pools, saying that former compliance officer Dana Richardson had written erroneous memos saying such pools were allowed. In regards to the "lack of institutional control" charge initially levied against Washington, the NCAA downgraded it to a "failure to monitor." It was tantamount to a slap on the wrist. Official recruiting visits from football recruits were reduced from 56 to 48 for the next two seasons. UW was also barred from using watercraft during recruiting, stemming from Neuheisel undercharging recruits for rides they received to and from his lakeside home. Ted Miller of the *Seattle-PI* wrote: "After more than 500 days of bluster, recrimination, legal wrangling, endless media opining and a good deal of despair from Huskies fans, the NCAA's case against Rick Neuheisel and the University of Washington concluded yesterday with the mildest of thuds."

Both Turner and UW President Mark Emmert felt relieved by the NCAA's findings. Turner believed the future to be bright, especially for his primary breadwinner—football. The previous year's graduation rate for the football team sat at 67%, second in the Pac-10 behind Stanford. The police blotter, which during the 2000 season contained the names of twelve football players, had cleared up to almost nothing. And Keith Gilbertson, the second-year coach who succeeded Neuheisel, had put together a recruiting class that Rivals.com ranked 19th best in the nation. Per Bud Withers of *The Seattle Times,* Turner expressed his optimism to an aide in the UW athletic department. "All is not broken at Washington," Turner said. "It's not in as bad shape as people in the country make it out to be. It's really in pretty good shape."

Of course, Turner couldn't have foreseen the train wreck that was to be the 2004 football season. By early November, team morale dipped as the losses piled up. Gilbertson began unloading on reporters in press conferences as he lost all control of the team. By season's end, the team's 1-10 record had made history of the worst kind.

The 2004 season snapped the string of 27 consecutive years without a losing record. Daily practice atmosphere had degenerated into angry screaming matches and a gloomy grind. As described by one player, "it was pretty much the players lining up for three to four hours and beating the shit out of each other."

During the season, Todd Turner had Gilbertson call Notre Dame's Tyrone Willingham to gauge his interest in the UW job. But now that Notre Dame had fired Willingham, Todd Turner couldn't have been more excited. He had long respected Willingham and once tried to lure him to Vanderbilt. Now, he had Willingham in his sights once again. Turner and Emmert flew to Chicago for a secret meeting with Willingham, and came away deeply impressed and incredulous he was available. Turner offered the job and Willingham accepted.

"For me, this was a very, very easy choice," Emmert said at the time. "When we sat down and talked to Tyrone, it couldn't have been clearer in my mind that this was the man we wanted to lead the University of Washington back to its former glory days. We were absolutely stunned and elated because we knew we had a chance to bring someone to the University of Washington who had all the characteristics we were looking for."

Tyrone Willingham overseeing a Husky football practice

CHAPTER 4

The Willingham Way

"I always keep in mind that coaches have an impact on the lives of youngsters. As a result, I am careful of what I might do in their sight. If someone saw me smoking a cigarette—which wouldn't happen since I don't smoke—but if I did, a youngster might think that meant it was okay for them to smoke. I think coaches should lead by example. Our young people don't need more sermons. They need more adults to look up to."

—Don James, former UW football coach,
in his 1990 autobiography

TYRONE Willingham's stoic public persona rendered him a blank canvas onto which people projected whatever they wanted to see. They'd see him on the sideline, during a game or around campus. Diminutive and nattily attired even if casually dressed, he didn't so much walk as march with his rigidly perfect posture and militaristic air. But it was that stoicism that bolstered his commanding presence. He looked you right in the eye while speaking in parables and quoted historical figures like Aristotle and Ghandi. One of his favorite phrases was "a word to the wise is sufficient."

Behind closed doors at Washington, Willingham wanted little to do with coaching.

When one of his former UW players was asked about Willingham's coaching ability, the player snapped: "I don't think Tyrone coached. He's not a smart coach, he's not an Xs and Os guy and he's not a recruiter. He's black. That's why they hired him. That's the only reason why. It was bullshit. Even the black players hated him."

Off-season workouts inside the Dempsey Center would find players sweating through intensive drills while Willingham spent countless hours practicing his golf swing. "He would always brag about being friends and playing golf with Tiger Woods," said defensive tackle Manase Hopoi. "We were like, okay, so what? None of us felt him on some of the things he talked about. He always talked about how Tiger Woods did all these things perfect, and so we needed to be like that. None of us got what he was getting at. Sometimes he would say his own son was a better athlete and a better man than all of us. It was always like he wanted to be putting somebody down. He didn't want anybody to be bigger than him, and was always pushing people away from him. We wanted to know him, how he grew up, but he didn't allow anybody to get to know him. Instead it was a lot of Tiger Woods stories. Okay, who cares? My uncle was the damn king of Tonga. So what? That's not who I am. So be a football coach, don't be Tiger Woods' friend."

Once the season started, Willingham scrapped the golf club but still maintained a detached air. While assistant coaches shouted instructions for their drills, Willingham chatted with visitors or wandered from drill to drill. Despite his national reputation as an offensive mastermind, dozens of former players stated they never received any instruction from him. "I don't ever recall him coaching," said Casey Paus. "Literally, I never remember him coaching any player on any aspect of the game. I'm wracking my brain and I don't remember seeing it even once. I feel like a lot of the staff weren't able to be themselves because of Willingham's conservative personality. There would be times in practice it would be, 'where the heck did he go?'"

The sounds of practice reverberated in Husky Stadium and the Dempsey Center indoor practice facility. The shouting of coaches, the thwacking of shoulder pads colliding, the blowing of whistles. Willingham would walk past drills and dispense inane advice like "hold onto the ball", "keep your head up" and "listen to your coaches." He also established himself as beyond reproach. "Willingham was extremely sensitive to criticism whenever anybody tried to ask him a question as to why," said one prominent former player. "There was always an attitude of players against coaches and of Willingham against the coaches. It was like Willingham was always on his own island."

Practices were not only tedious, they also sapped the team of the energy needed on game day. "People always wondered why Willingham teams collapsed in the second half," said a former player. "It was because there was no fucking common sense used to structure the practices."

Former linebacker Scott White, now a linebacker coach at Palomar College in California, went into greater detail. "The way practice was structured, I always wondered why we were in pads on Thursday. As anyone in football knows, as the week goes by, you're supposed to tail it back and get into game mode. Mentally putting a polish on it, being sharp, knowing the looks you're going to get. But Willingham's coaches turned Thursdays into 9 on 7 drills, goal line reps and goal line packages. I distinctly remember getting into games and my legs were tired. My legs were heavy. It was a culmination of the week.

"On Saturday you play 70 snaps, and then on Sundays you're back out there you have to run 350 meters around the field after you played the day before," said White. "The idea was to get the lactic acid and stiffness out and that's true. But it fatigues you, and the body needs time to recover. It's a known fact. Monday was supposed to be that recovery day but you're in school and doing a bunch of stuff, and then you're right back out there at practice on Tuesday. When are you ever going to recover? That's why Willingham's team had those long losing streaks every season. It's because the team was worn out by the end of the year. It was inevitable as each season wore on. You saw the same thing when he was at Notre Dame, how they would fade."

While practices wore the players out physically, team meetings often wore them out mentally. Players would assemble in the team room as Willingham entered and marched to the front. "There would be four team meetings a week," said a prominent former player. "They were a fucking joke. We would talk about the other team for thirty minutes every week. It was all done up on PowerPoint. He loved that stupid, fucking PowerPoint clicker. He carried it with him everywhere he went. He would tell us what station was televising the game, where in the country it would be seen, and that we had an opportunity to win a game. He would tell us the projected weather report. Thursday would be the same thing, almost word-for-word. Fridays were *the worst.*

We would get a detailed weather report and a parable. It would take 20-30 minutes. We would be sitting there going HOLY SHIT. He would read us quotes from Muhammad Ali. We would be thinking, 'We don't care about what Muhammad Ali says. We want to know how you're going to lead us to win a football game!'"

The strangest part of meetings would come at the end. Tyrone Willingham regularly conducted research into his players' lives, and his findings came to light during team meetings. "He'd sometimes have papers in his hand," said safety Chris Hemphill. "He had MySpace comments printed out. He would say: 'Guys, what are you doing? Come on, clean up your MySpace pages.' I felt like it wasn't necessary. If guys are doing everything they are supposed to and want to have a couple beers in their down time, it's nobody's business. It's not like we were drunk and unruly. I never had a MySpace, but guys weren't happy about that. I felt like it would have been better to talk to guys one-on-one instead of putting their business out there for the whole team to hear."

Safety C.J. Wallace likened the meetings to a stepfather addressing his stepchildren. "We weren't allowed to curse, especially on the field," said Wallace. "It was kind of funny and kind of weird. I think we might have been the best-speaking team in the nation. If there was a Heisman Trophy for being a good speaker, they missed somebody on our team.

"And he would pop up on us in class a lot," continued Wallace. "Everybody expects a little bit of privacy and he overstepped his boundaries a little bit. For the guys old enough to drink, they would be down at The Ram from time to time. Willingham showed up there a few times and told the bartender to stop serving the players drinks."

"He would know who you hung out with, and it was like his coaching staff was the FBI," added Scott White. "It had nothing to do with football or school. He would read comments online or cite a picture of someone at a party. He would give the message to clean up your Myspace pages. I don't know what made him get on it, but it was stuff that I've never seen anywhere else in my time as a coach. He would have gotten a lot further by coming in and believing in his players and doing things the right way."

Meanwhile, former players were catching glimpses of what was happening and several didn't like what they saw. In the spring of 2006, the Big W Club put together a BBQ that would co-mingle current and former players. The former players gathered first to be introduced to Willingham. After several minutes of delay following the malfunction of a projector, Willingham gave up and opened the floor to questions. A player from the 1960s raised his hand and asked gruffly, "When are you going to get rid of that weasel-ass logo and turn it back into a mean tough Husky and get back to hitting people?"

Willingham began speaking in the third person. "Well, Coach Willingham is looking into it. Coach Willingham is considering de-emphasizing that logo and making the Husky W more prominent."

Then someone else asked, "When I see USC on TV, the cameras pan the sideline and there's Marcus Allen, Ronnie Lott and Anthony Munoz. How come they are welcome there but nobody here can get a sideline pass and feel a part of Husky football?"

"Coach Willingham is working on that."

"We were sitting there going OH MY GOD, ARE YOU KIDDING ME?" said a player from the 1978 Rose Bowl team. "This is our coach? Then we went up and had a meal with the current players. We were all saying THIS FOOL IS OUR COACH? I knew right then that it was a bad deal. I said to myself, it's not going to end well."

For many former Huskies, Willingham's presence as UW coach was puzzling. For others, it was downright infuriating. "I will argue until the end of time that he never would have gotten the Washington job if he wasn't black," said another former Husky and NFL veteran, "because he never would have coached Stanford, which means he never would have coached Notre Dame. The guy was never a coordinator. If he was a white guy there's isn't a chance in hell he would have got the Stanford job. The Stanford and Notre Dame alums believed that Willingham could go into the middle class black homes in America, and he could bring them to their school.

"But you have to look at Willingham's background. The guy was never a coordinator. When you're a coordinator, you have your nuts on the line. He was a running backs coach. Running back coach is the lowest and most meaningless coaching position in the NFL. You hand the football to a back, and he either knows how to run the ball or not. If there's one position that doesn't need a coach in pro football, it's a running back. He was a fucking running backs coach. There is no way that you become a head coach from there unless you're black."

W

Former Husky Jamal Fountaine (photo by Staci Fountaine)

CHAPTER 5

A Visit with Jamal Fountaine

Jamal Fountaine was a Bay Area linebacker who played for the Washington Huskies during the team's glory years of the early 1990s. Three times his teams went to the Rose Bowl and the 1991 squad won a share of the National Championship. Jamal was a captain on the 1993 team. He then signed with San Francisco and was on the roster when the 49ers won the 1995 Super Bowl. Following two seasons with the Atlanta Falcons, he retired due to injuries. He subsequently went into construction management and then worked as an assistant coach for Portland State. Today he's a firefighter in the Bay Area and married with two kids.

When looking back to what drew him to Seattle, Fountaine recalled being ditched at a party by his UW recruiting host, linebacker Chico Fraley. While standing on a street corner, Fountaine became engrossed in a conversation with "this regular common dude, grungy guy." The guy had no idea who Fountaine was, and Fountaine appreciated speaking to someone who wasn't trying to sell him on the school.

"He told me that they were tough no matter how bad the record was," Fountaine said. "They would knock the crap out of you."

Derek Johnson: What were your thoughts when Tyrone Willingham was hired as the Husky coach in December 2004?

Fountaine: I was really excited when he got signed by the University of Washington. I thought it was historic in many different ways. I didn't think the school would ever hire a black football coach. And then to go out and get a black football coach of his magnitude at that time, with the success he had at Stanford and then considering how poorly Notre Dame treated him by releasing him so quickly from his contract. For U-Dub to pick him up was great. I thought he would be great as far as recruiting higher quality student athletes considering his history at Stanford and Notre Dame. And the thought that he could go out recruiting in the Midwest and utilize some of the ties that he had out there.

But when he came on and assembled his staff, with the exception of Chris Tormey and Randy Hart, they were a bunch of people who didn't have any ties to the Northwest and didn't care about the Northwest. And very arrogant, you know?

Johnson: Are we talking about people like defensive coordinator Kent Baer?

Fountaine: I thought Kent Baer was an asshole. In my opinion he was not a good person. Now, I speak as someone who has been involved in football as a player and coach for 25 years. I attended many of the Washington practices and my brother Matt was a redshirt sophomore defensive back when Willingham got there. I would stand there and listen to Baer and wonder what in the hell is this guy saying? I thought his system was too complicated for the kids and it changed week to week. It had no fundamental base.

Johnson: What were your early impressions of Willingham?

Fountaine: Within three to four weeks of seeing this guy, watching his practices, listening to him talk to these kids, I knew there was going to be a disconnect between him and his players. I didn't feel like that was the way that teachers should be. I was like, whoa, my brother is here, I hope he doesn't get caught up in this. I didn't know how he was going to fit in with that.

And I know that people always talk about how Tyrone was dealing with Neuheisel recruits. But no matter what people think about Neuheisel and [defensive coordinator] Tim Hundley, those guys were teachers. They taught kids instead of directing kids. There's a huge difference. There's a football teacher and there's a director. And I recognized immediately that Willingham's philosophy was that he needed to get the current players out of there and get his players in there. I knew that was going to be the thing.

I was looking at this from the outside and from having been a coach, and from having gone to multiple practices and listening to the things my brother was telling me. I saw what was going on and I didn't think there was any teaching going on.

I can't compare Willingham to Don James or any other coach I've worked for because I thought there was a huge disconnect. But I understood a lot of the things of what Tyrone Willingham was trying to instill. And a lot of things could be helpful to those kids down the line. But I don't think he was ever telling the kids that. And they are kids—that's the thing. They're fragile. As big and as strong as they are, football players are probably some of the most fragile people on the planet. And their egos are inflated because they are insecure. And I know that Tyrone Willingham understands that, because he's a very intelligent man. He's a man with a great plan and a great vision. But I don't think he has a great way of communicating it to the players. Or maybe the people he communicated to at Stanford and Notre Dame understood that, but for these kids at Washington, it's never been that way. To my knowledge, no coach at Washington has ever had that type of vision for the players. That culture was so different that I don't think these kids could even begin to understand where he was coming from. But for African-American men it was the right thing for him to try to do.

Johnson: Please go into that deeper.

Fountaine: Well I was thirteen years removed since I had played at UW. But Willingham's primary emphasis was to go to class, to sit in the front of the class. To wear collared shirts. To be a participant in the class. Those things were revolutionary. Those things weren't being said when I was in school. It wasn't like they said don't go to class. But they would say: If you don't go to class we're going to run you (*laughs*). If you don't get good grades, we're going to run you. Coach Hart did class checks on us and all that kind of stuff, but he was covering his ass to make sure his players were eligible. And I say that in emphasizing that Coach Hart cared. But they weren't trying to teach you about the real world with that.

If players major in rock for jocks, there won't be any jobs for them after they're done playing. Even after the NFL, there won't be any job for you after you're done. There won't be a job for you and you will struggle. And if you look at the majority of people who played college football they end up struggling because they have degrees they can't market. And that's the problem with the NCAA, and that's a huge problem.

So Tyrone came in saying hey it's my duty as a black coach for all the kids, but primarily for the black kids, is that you cannot go into corporate America with cornrows in your hair, gold teeth and sagging [pants]. You can't do that, so don't think you can do that here. And so when the kids heard that, they did what most kids would do, and that's rebel.

Johnson: When I was interviewing C.J. Wallace, I asked him if there was anything about Willingham that he respected. C.J. said that Willingham gave him a greater appreciation for his education.

Fountaine: Yeah, well it should be the coach's job to just graduate players, but it's convoluted because there's pressure to win. But he was also coaching at a school that didn't want to be big-time. They just don't. The University of Washington of today has no desire to be a big-time football program. Tyrone's message was complex. The way he went about it was so radically different that it alienated everybody. But if you talk to guys that have been out of the system for awhile you can ask them: was what he was telling you the truth?

But you know, players have got to take ownership too. Back when I was in college and we were playing Stanford, my coach got pissed at me for saying that to the media. A reporter asked me if I was worried about going up against Bill Walsh. And I said Bill Walsh doesn't make plays. Once the game starts he isn't out there. Same for Tyrone Willingham. Yeah he can call a time out, yeah he can override a call, yeah he can put a player in. But when the damn whistle blows and the ball is snapped, it becomes the players. And if your players, truthfully, are smoking weed, getting high, chasing broads and not serious about the game, then it becomes the players' fault. It ain't the coaches' fault. It ain't. But we all understand that the coaches get fired for poor performances and that's the way it is.

But you know that many of these kids aren't serious about the game until they get paid for it. There are some that see themselves as ball players. But out of 85 kids, how many will that be?

Johnson: Go into that some more.

Fountaine: These kids are very much immersed in the college life. No matter how many rules they put on them to separate them from the others on campus, like be here at 5:30 AM and study table and all that, the fact of the matter is that these are just kids, man. They are 18-23 years old and they have different focuses. Some of them love football, some of them still play football for their parents. It's rare to get kids to come to school to be serious enough to handle the information Tyrone was throwing on them.

Now tack on the whole aspect of "The Willingham Way", and talking about himself in the third person. That was a little strange, I agree. It was strange and we would have said the same thing if Coach James had been talking about himself in the third person (*laughs*). But in his own way Coach James told us we needed to do things his way. He made it clear it was his way or the highway. We didn't have all the options the kids have today, man (*laughs*). We didn't have any rights!

Johnson: Your former teammate Dave Hoffmann tells me that even headphones were not allowed on the bus and plane.

Fountaine: Please! No talking and no headphones. It was a business trip. We were all business. These cats today get the headphones and all these distractions. It's a whole different game. I was very disappointed in my brother's experience at the University of Washington. But it taught him a lot about the life that is going to happen and the life I have experienced since then. The false realities and hard realities that will come to him post-football. He didn't have the football success that I had, which was a shame. But he learned a lot about the harsh realities of life.

Caesar Rayford pursues Washington State quarterback

CHAPTER 6

A Visit with Caesar Rayford

Caesar Rayford was a 6'7" 245 pound defensive end who played sparingly in his four years at Washington, recording only 13 tackles in that entire time. After leaving Seattle, Rayford became a member of the B.C. Lions of the Canadian Football League. Coach and General Manager Wally Buono turned heads when he speculated about Rayford's lack of development at Washington under Willingham. "It amazes me they couldn't develop a player of his natural ability with the facilities they have there," Buono said. "If they had done this when he was 17, 18, 19, 20, look what he might have become. We did it in less than a year. If he had been at this point when he was 20, we'd probably be watching him on TV [in the NFL]."

Derek Johnson: What kind of problems did you see crop up when Willingham arrived at Washington?

Caesar Rayford: The one thing that threw things off was when Willingham took the name off the jerseys and put us in colors that made us look like Notre Dame. We were the Huskies, and we wondered why we were being made to look like Notre Dame. It was discouraging to see him removing our traditions like that. There were many little changes, and it was like our whole persona was changed. Willingham felt like everything we had been doing was unnecessary. We were looking at each other going, "If we're not the Huskies anymore, then who are we?"

Another thing was the firing of one of our strength coaches, Steve Emtman. How do you send away Steve Emtman? He was somebody that had so much success and brought so much to the University of

Washington. How do you force out someone like that? Through his weight program, I gained weight and got much stronger. Our weight room was so motivated with Emtman. We called it Club Weight Room. We were so excited to go there and lift weights. And then Willingham gets rid of Emtman and brings in Trent Greener. Everybody hated him. And right away, everybody got weaker and weaker. Numbers started dropping immediately. We went to Willingham and said this isn't working. Willingham said he wasn't changing nothing.

Johnson: You said before that those were some pretty rough times for you at Washington.

Rayford: It was discouraging, because every time I went out there I always made plays. I stayed within the system and worked my tail off but I felt like I never got rewarded. Greyson Gunheim was ahead of me and he was a great player. But even when I made plays, in the following weeks I wouldn't get much time on the field. I would talk to the coaches and say 'How do I get onto the field?' They would say 'Gain weight, gain weight, gain weight.' So I would stay all summer and work out, and in mat drills I would basically beat out everybody. But once the season started, I would be on the sidelines. It came to the point, as part of the Willingham system, where I became silent and just waited for the times that I would be told to go onto the field and then bust my tail.

And my frustration wasn't just in regards to myself. I watched a lot of guys work their tails off and guys leave their blood and sweat out on the field, and their careers or scholarships would be taken away from them for reasons nobody understood. It was most devastating for the guys that never got any chance to play. We're talking about very talented guys that are working hard in mat drills, competing to get better, being good teammates. I mean, this isn't the NFL, this is college. How can you do that to young people's futures?

Johnson: And how would guys like that respond?

Rayford: For the most part guys would just become silent and would be just like whatever. Because I mean, at a certain point what can you do?

Johnson: At the end of the 2006 season in the Apple Cup, you made the final tackle of the game. A sack of the Cougar quarterback to preserve the win for the Huskies. It was your only tackle for the season.

Rayford: I hadn't played much. But when Brandon Ala got hurt they put Chris Stevens in. I was begging and pleading with the coaches, 'Put me in! Put me in! Put me in! I will make a play. Give me a chance!' And they finally said alright get in there. On the last play I lined up and sacked the Washington State quarterback at the end of the game.

Johnson: C.J. Wallace told me that that game felt like the Super Bowl to the players.

Rayford: As players that's all we had. It was our Super Bowl, that was our bowl game, it was our everything. We said this is our game, not the coaches'. It belongs to us. There was great happiness in the locker room afterwards. Oh it was a celebration. We were celebrating like we had just won the BCS Championship game. Given everything that happened to us that season, to have it end like that was phenomenal. That game was largely won by people that weren't starters or had been on the back burner all season. We were loose instead of tight.

Johnson: Was there a feeling among players like if they made a mistake there would be hell to pay?

Rayford: Oh yeah, I can speak from personal experience. That's how it was for me. It got to the point where I played so timid. I was already limited in playing time as it was, so I knew if I made a mistake I would be pulled from the game. So people would play kind of content. You're out there, and you're thinking 'Don't make a mistake, don't make a mistake, don't make a mistake…' Then you would make one and be pulled from the game. Then you're hanging your head on the sideline and going ughhhh.

We were so worried that we would tense up. Willingham took the fire out of us. When we were with Coach Gilbertson I felt like there was some fire in the team. But when Willingham came in, I remember that a little fight broke out on the field, and he made the whole team run a mile in pads. It was like he wanted to remove the aggressiveness from us.

Johnson: That reminds me of the 2007 game at Oregon State. Beaver safety Al Alfalava had the hard hit on Jake Locker that knocked him out of the game. All of a sudden, the Huskies seemed upset and lineman Ryan Tolar got into a scuffle and got ejected. It seemed like the team was going to rise up and go to war, but then everything died out. Oregon State hung on and won the game.

Rayford: We were pissed off and we were ready to go after them. But Willingham told us no, we will never do anything like that. It was one of those times when we would get some fire and then he would immediately tap it out. Just like when the Cougars stomped on our W after the 2005 game. That was our house. You protect your W. It's like somebody pissing on your couch. When they did that you don't stand for it. And for Willingham to publicly apologize for our behavior, they should have been the ones apologizing. Regardless of what happened in the game, you don't do that. They want to dance on our W, so we retaliated. That's our house and we'll come after you. And then Willingham got mad at us! You're going to get mad at us? That's your field as much as it is ours! That's our sanctuary. That's our blood and sweat that's on that field. Why do you care more about apologizing to your opponent than defending your home and your players?

Johnson: Did things change that day for the team?

Rayford: Everything did change that day for us. I feel like we went from the Dawgs to the puppies. We became timid. Football is a fight. Football is a violent, physical sport. And that got taken away. It got to the point where guys loathed practice and it was like here we go again… Here we go again…. Here we go again…

I talked to guys from around the Pac-10. When I was with the BC Lions [in 2008], my roommate was Jeremy Gibbs who played at Oregon. You know how the rivalry between Washington and Oregon was always nasty for years and years? Jeremy said that he looked forward to playing us but then it was like we were just out there going through the motions. He said he felt like he was in practice with his teammates.

He said that the Ducks knew they would walk all over us for as long as Willingham was there.

When it comes to football, there's nothing nice going on. It is two teams trying to kick the crap out of each other. There's not a place for being out there trying to be nice guys. At least with Gilbertson, as badly as we struggled in 2004, I felt like we still had some attitude. But Willingham removed all attitude and burning fire. Every time we tried to get it back, he would come and take it away.

Johnson: Was there anything positive you took from Willingham?

Rayford: Willingham had a lot of values to make us better as men. He brought in people to help us to build a resume and things to help with our career building. For life after football. He brought in people to talk to us. He gave us a lot of stuff to make us better as men. He just forgot to focus on football.

Skyline High School All-American quarterback Jake Heaps

CHAPTER 7

The Lazy Recruiter

"Hard work spotlights the character of people: some turn up their sleeves, some turn up their noses, and some don't turn up at all."

—Sam Ewing, writer

"A lot of coaches complain about recruiting," said former UW coach Don James in his 1990 autobiography. "I have never felt that way. It's a good thing because it is probably the single most important thing we coaches do... The challenge of recruiting is that something needs rebuilding every year—offensive backs, defensive line receivers, defensive backs."

In the eighteen years James coached at Washington, the recruiting season meant watching countless hours of game film, traveling thousands of miles to visit recruits and burning the midnight oil. To be an outstanding recruiter meant aggressively going the extra mile. One of James' favorite stories stemmed from a time he recruited a player from California. As James pulled his rental car up to the recruit's house, the boy suddenly ran out the front door, jumped into his own car, and took off at high speed. James stayed right behind him. The two cars weaved through the hills of San Pedro. James had no idea where they were until the kid pulled up in front of a house which ended up belonging to his high school coach.

It turned out that a coach from another school had changed his mind the night before and was scheduled to arrive there in a few minutes and sign the player to a letter of intent. Seeing he was outnumbered, James re-started the recruiting process, going over a checklist comparison of the two schools. The youngster acknowledged that Washington was superior on every front. James told him he was leaving and would be back in two hours. When James returned exactly two hours later, the young man signed his letter of intent with Washington.

Don James and his staff earned a reputation among high school football coaches as hard-working and diligent. Conversely, prep coaches did not hold Tyrone Willingham in the same regard. One Seattle-area coach saw one of his players return from a recruiting trip to Washington feeling befuddled. Willingham told the player: "You need to make the decision for yourself. We're not going to call you every week. If you want to come here, it's because you want to. You need to make this decision on your own. We're not going to hold your hand through the process." The youngster ended up singing with another Pac-10 school when most people thought he was destined to be a Husky.

During the Willingham era at Washington, this pattern repeated itself *ad nauseum.* The Huskies were suddenly duking it out with inferior programs like Idaho, Fresno State and Utah State on a regular basis. A bevy of big-time blue chippers left the state for other schools. Jonathan Stewart went to Oregon, Taylor Mays selected USC, Anthony Felder picked California, Steve Schilling bounded for Michigan, and Jake Heaps headed to BYU.

Many fans and media chalked up the misfortune to the notion that Washington was a massive rebuilding project. In truth, Willingham's neglect on the recruiting trail doomed hopes of landing quality classes. For reasons no one understood, Willingham seemed reticent to challenge powerhouse schools directly for top talent. Steve Schilling and Jake Heaps were poignant examples. Schilling, a stud lineman from powerhouse Bellevue, grew up a lifelong Husky fan. All that knew him considered his matriculating at Washington a slam dunk. Willingham was even told by Bellevue coaches: "All you have to do is call Steve regularly during the recruiting process and tell him you want him at Washington, and he's yours."

But by halfway through Schilling's senior season, he'd received very little communication from Washington. Meanwhile, other major programs like USC, UCLA, Cal and Michigan were pursuing aggressively. USC Trojan coach Pete Carroll was personally calling Schilling once a week for the entire season.

When Schilling told his high school coach Butch Goncharoff of his intention of going to Michigan, Goncharoff was stunned and asked why. Schilling shrugged and said he hadn't heard from Washington in several weeks and figured they'd dumped him. When a perplexed Goncharoff tracked down Willingham to find out why, the UW coach replied: "We're in the middle of our football schedule. We will call Stephen at the end of the season."

A similar scenario played out with Skyline High School's Jake Heaps, heralded by multiple recruiting evaluators as the top quarterback in the country. Massive media attention focused upon the likable young man. He narrowed his choices down to BYU and Washington before selecting BYU. But an anonymous source close to the Heaps family portrayed a horrific picture behind the recruiting scenes. "A lot of people think it was a done deal because Jake was Latter Day Saints that he was going to BYU," said the source. "What people don't know is that Jake's father is one of the biggest Husky fans around. When he went to a Husky basketball game with [UW assistant] Doug Nussmeier, he was rattling off all the great Husky basketball and football player names going all the way back to when he was a kid. Jake's family really wanted him to go to UW but in the end BYU had developed a relationship and recruited him the hardest and the best. Going into Jake's junior year, Tennessee, LSU, Florida and USC all came by. Those schools from far away came by more frequently than Washington did—and Willingham lived near our school. His own son played for the team."

The source added: "When Steve Sarkisian and Doug Nussmeier came on board in 2009, they brought everything they could but it was just too late in the process. The commitment to recruit Jake wasn't there until Sark got there. Holy cow was it different. They had a coach there every time they legally could. Jake liked Sark immensely. If Sark had another four months, he absolutely would have gotten Jake to go to Washington."

Willingham's cold indifference also extended to prep coaching staffs. A Seattle-area coach lamented how Willingham kept him at arm's length. "He wasn't very open to high school coaches coming in and sitting in meetings," he said. "Same for watching video with the UW staff or using their resources. We had flown to Northwestern, Oregon, Texas, Washington State, and they would always say: 'Here's a room and you can have access to anything you want.' But with Willingham, it was frustrating. I asked Willingham in person if I could sit in receiver meetings. He said to me abruptly that I couldn't. He said it would be a distraction to his team. I said I would just be a fly on the wall and won't ask any questions or anything, but he said I couldn't do that."

Be it by fiat or example, Willingham's work ethic trickled down through the coaching staff. One January evening—when recruiting was in high gear—a major UW booster wandered into the coaches' offices. He encountered linebacker coach and recruiting coordinator Chris Tormey heading out the door. The booster looked at his watch and saw that it was only 6:30PM, but the building was virtually empty. When the booster asked Tormey where he was going, Tormey explained he had errands to run and then needed to get home. Gone were the days when the staffs of Don James, Jim Lambright and Rick Neuheisel worked sixteen hour days. "Was it any wonder recruiting was going so badly?" the booster mused. "You can't compete with the big time programs by working forty-hour work weeks."

Willingham and his staff did land a handful of notable recruits. Quarterback Jake Locker, linebacker Mason Foster and running back Chris Polk come to mind. Of course, Locker later indicated he was likely coming to Washington regardless of the coach. And it turned out Chris Polk and several others in the class of 2008 came to Washington when a desperate Willingham promised them they would start instantly.

"I think Willingham's a good person and has good morals," said an area high school coach. "I think he did his best to really shape young men and I don't think you can fault him for any of that. The word was that he was very good with families and making them feel like their son was in good hands. So it wasn't all negative. But the recruiting and the way he carried himself around the media could have been a lot better. Along with wins on the field, it would have served him a lot better to have been more personable."

W

Washington wide receiver Craig Chambers

CHAPTER 8

A Visit with Craig Chambers

Coming out of Jackson high school in Mill Creek, WA, Craig Chambers was one of the crown jewels in Rick Neuheisel's final recruiting class at Washington. Recruiting expert Tom Lemming tabbed Chambers as the 15th best wide receiver in America for the 2003 class, while SuperPrep magazine anointed Chambers the 4th best player in the state of Washington.

Chambers was a legacy recruit at Washington, as his brother Richie had been a hard-hitting linebacker back in the early 1990s when Washington owned a dominant presence throughout college football. At 6'3" and 205 pounds, Chambers was rangy with deceptive speed. He possessed a breath-taking ability to go up in traffic and pull down great catches. He also marched to the beat of his own drum, and drew consternation from coaches by sometimes dropping passes in practice. Following the 2005 season, Chambers abruptly transferred from Division I Washington to Division II Montana. To this day, not a week goes by that someone doesn't ask him why he would ever leave the Huskies, and many chalked it up to Willingham removing more proverbial cancer from the team.

Derek Johnson: What was it like when you became a Husky?

Craig Chambers: I pretty much knew I was going to be a Husky when I was younger. Having Gilbertson there was nice because he had been a coach there when my brother was there. Steve Emtman was also there and played with my brother. When I signed with U-Dub in 2003, we were still one of the top teams in the Pac-10. We were ranked ahead of USC. Cody Pickett was ranked high as a QB, and Reggie Williams was a Heisman Trophy candidate. I don't know why but everything started to fall apart toward the end of 2003.

Johnson: In your redshirt freshman season in 2004, the offense was really struggling when you suddenly made your first start against Oregon down at Autzen Stadium in Eugene.

Chambers: The Friday night before the game at our team hotel, I talked to [assistant coach] Steve Axman. I told him "Hey, our receivers are struggling. I don't know why I drop balls in practice, but if you give me a chance, I can make a difference." Axman went and talked to coach Gilbertson, and then came back and said "you're starting!" I was like, "huh?" But what better place to start for a guy who grew up loving the Huskies than Autzen Stadium against the Ducks. It was on TV, it was a dream come true.

The game was so fast, everything was going a million miles an hour. A former Husky came up to me on the sideline, I don't remember who it was, but he said "Hey you look flustered. Try to chill." That talk settled me down, and I had my coming out party. And for the last four games of the season I had 19 catches and 400+ yards. That was a good time for me. I had been waiting for fourteen years to do that. It was a long time coming.

Johnson: At the end of that season, the Huskies went 1-10 for their first losing season in 28 years. Gilbertson was fired and Tyrone Willingham was brought in as the next coach. What were your thoughts?

Chambers: That 2004 season was rough. When you go to college you go there to be successful. It's your dream and aspiration to at least win a bowl. My brother played on the national championship team and in three Rose Bowls. Conversely, I played on the worst Washington team of all time. So that was tough.

I hadn't watched Notre Dame so I didn't know much about them. All I knew was that he had been fired. Why would you hire someone that just got fired? The way I looked at it, what wasn't good enough for Notre Dame was good enough to Washington. Why would UW lower its standards? They fired him for a reason. Why would we take their scraps? UW is still an elite program. If we turn things around, we will sell out the stadium and make millions of dollars. So why lower your standards like that? It didn't make sense.

Johnson: How was your relationship with Willingham?

Chambers: We got off on the wrong foot. He came and acted like he was better than us. I grew up loving Husky football. I still love the Huskies and watch every game. Some people have other opinions and think that I am a traitor, but I don't care what they think. I come from a Husky family and it's very important. When he came in and changed everything, I took that real personal. Willingham is a very arrogant dude. During morning workouts he would swing his golf club. Dude, really?

Then in January, I was at [teammate] Chris Rohrbach's house. My mom called me and said that dad had passed away. He died from internal bleeding. He was on kidney dialysis. He got these lumps that were blood clots on his arm where the needle pierces the skin. One of them burst and they thought he was going to be fine. They sent him to the University of Washington hospital. That's where he died. I had to claim his body at the hospital.

The hospital is right next to Husky Stadium. It was too much to see it every day. It quickly changed the whole atmosphere of U-Dub for me. If you want to get over something, it makes it harder when you face it every day. It's like if you see a family member murdered in your house, you're probably going to move.

Johnson: This occurred during winter conditioning?

Chambers: Yes, I had been away for five days when I got a call from Liz, who was Willingham's assistant. She said that Coach Willingham wanted me back at practice. I said fine, no problem, that's okay.

Two days later I was there for a team meeting. It was seven days after my dad had passed away. Willingham was standing in front of the whole team in the team room. He said, "I question the toughness of this football team." He called out Louis Rankin. Louis was a running back and he was dealing with turf toe. For anyone dealing with turf toe, you know that it feels like you've got a broken toe. Willingham said: "People suffer injuries all the time; it's no excuse to miss practice… Family members pass away; it's no excuse to miss practice." And for me that was that. I couldn't play for him anymore. I was ready to say fuck you Willingham. But it was too late to transfer so I knew I would have to wait out the 2005 season and then transfer.

Johnson: While waiting for the 2005 season, you saw your assistant strength coach Steve Emtman leave the program. What were your thoughts?

Chambers: After Willingham came in, Steve Emtman was really the only guy left from the old guard, except Randy Hart who never spoke to the offensive guys. Emtman was cool and he knew what he was doing. He had the ability to give us an identity. He had won a national championship. On the sideline, he would shout "this is fucking pathetic!", but the way he went about it, we listened to him. He was like Coach Yarber, he cared about us. He wasn't there for the money. How could Willingham fire a guy like that?

Johnson: Then came the 2005 season. Given your performance in 2004, it was hard to understand why you weren't on the first string for the opener against Air Force. There was speculation in the papers about your absence on the field.

Chambers: Even before our first day of spring practice, Willingham put me on second string. Without even looking at me in practice. But the Air Force game pissed me off. I wanted to throw the table over in the locker room. He didn't play me the whole game. We were ahead in the fourth but then we fell behind with about a minute to go. That's when he put me in the game. That added insult to injury, like he knew I could do it. Like I could make a big play. That was the point where I lost all respect for him. If you're going to sit me out, then sit me out the whole game. Don't put me in for the last minute because you need something done.

Johnson: The following week, your mom made an infamous call into KJR sports radio. She complained about your playing time and hinted that you might transfer if it didn't improve.

Chambers: Ah, yes. That was not my finest hour. I never heard it but someone told me, "hey your mom was on KJR complaining about your playing time." I asked Mom if she called KJR. At first she said no. I said "Mom?" And she admitted she had done so. At the time I was pissed, and didn't speak to her for two weeks.

Johnson: The conclusion of the 2005 season brought with it the chance to transfer. You chose Division II Montana, meaning you could play without sitting out a season.

Chambers: I felt like the shadows were closing in on me, and I had to get away. I have heard a million different versions of why I left. I still hear it almost daily. They don't always recognize me, but when they hear my name, they say, "Oh you're that receiver. You were doing so good, why did you go to Montana?" But I wanted to live in peace and go start a new chapter somewhere else.

Montana was cool, they take good care of you over there. Awesome town, they love their Grizzlies. Great game day atmosphere. When you're in Seattle, there's over two million people. Probably 85% don't even care about Husky football. I'm sure 50% of them aren't even from Seattle. U-Dub is not a college, it's a university. If you want a college atmosphere, you need to go to a college town. In Montana, there are caricatures of you on every single business's window. For real. On game day, there are three gas stations and they have a bidding to decide which one will stay open so the other two can close and go to the games. The stadium holds 30,000 people, but there would be 100,000 around the stadium tailgating and being a part of the experience. I love Washington, but it's just different.

Johnson: How did your Montana career go?

Chambers: I had some success but then I blew out my shoulder. I didn't get to play my senior year. My shoulder is still numb to this day.

Johnson: Sorry to hear that.

Chambers: But I took it as a blessing. It got me started on my life earlier than I would have been. I went ahead and started my own business. In life you have a choice to look at things as opportunities or as something that will hold you back.

Johnson: In looking back, what's your assessment of the coaching you got at Washington?

Chambers: There was definitely a divide between coaches and players. Coach [Eric] Yarber was one of the best I had in my life. He was awesome. He cared about his players. He wants you to be successful for the sake of you being successful, not so it will make him look good. Lots of times, coaches only root for your success so they can keep their jobs. On the inside, you can see a coach start to crumble when things go bad. You can see the things going on inside of them. There's a lot of money at stake. Players can see through this stuff, they really can. I think that's why Pete Carroll did so well, is that he cared about his players. His players say he's a good dude. And you can be a mean coach, too. But if you care about your players, you can inspire them to do great things. I don't think Willingham cared that much about his players.

W

Safety C.J. Wallace is all smiles after Huskies beat Washington State in his final college game

CHAPTER 9

A Visit with C. J. Wallace

Even before the age of two, C.J. Wallace stood out as a great athlete. He could zip a tiny tot football across the living room with a perfect spiral. If a sports game was on, "Little C.J." would quietly disappear, before returning moments later with the appropriate ball. The family always laughed at these antics, made even more comical by the serious and nonplussed look on C.J.'s face as he studied the flashing screen and mimicked what he saw.

But it wasn't until C.J. turned three that his parents realized football was closest to his heart. When his mom took him to get a studio portrait taken, the photographer tried various tricks of the trade to get the kid to smile. C.J. remained non-expressive as he looked into the camera and the photos clicked away. His mom finally saved the day when she suggested that her son be given a football to hold. The boy's face lit up with a big smile.

For the next two decades Wallace was a quiet leader on every football team he joined. He was ultimately recognized as an All Pac-10 safety at the University of Washington. Upon graduating, he entered the NFL in 2007 and played three seasons with the Seattle Seahawks. In 2010, he was a member of the UFL Champion Las Vegas Locomotives.

Derek Johnson: By the time Tyrone Willingham came to Washington, you had already played for head coaches Rick Neuheisel and Keith Gilbertson. What were your early impressions?

Wallace: I didn't really know what to think. I didn't really expect him to be picked as the coach since he got fired from Notre Dame. I always thought of Tyrone Willingham as a military person and that's how he was when he first came in. It seemed like he came in trying to make a whole lot of strange rules. Maybe he had reasons to behave that way, having just been fired from Notre Dame. He tried to do too much. It seemed like we were just there to go to school. I didn't really feel the attitude of winning coming from him.

Johnson: Teammates of yours have told me that players were aware of Willingham making comments both in private and publicly that there wasn't much talent on the roster.

Wallace: I remember guys coming through the locker room with the newspaper and people talking about things he said. I thought he was crazy. With our guys, I felt like we had a good team that had had one tough season [in 2004]. I didn't feel like it was that hard for Tyrone Willingham to come in and coach our team.

Many of us knew we were going to the NFL. Everything that Tyrone said we disagreed upon. We was never really on the same page. One minute he would go to the media saying negative stuff, then he would come back and try to make us believe in ourselves. A lot of guys didn't want to play for him. Nobody wanted to follow.

He always talked in the third person. He would say: "If you do it the Willingham Way this, the Willingham way that, we're going to be champions." Then he'd go to the media and say negative things. You can't lead like that. He said we had the worst athletes he's ever seen, and then he comes back and says if we do it his way we're going to be champions.

Johnson: Was it difficult playing under those conditions?

Wallace: It made me turn into a selfish player, because I began saying that I was going to be out for mine. Even though I was a team player and I loved my teammates, I didn't want anything stopping me from competing [in the NFL]. I always went out there and gave it my all and competed against myself. I didn't want to be that way but I knew I had to be that way.

It helped me play to the maximum level and my teammates loved me for that. I never left my college career feeling any doubt about that, because we wasn't winning, but at the same time you can't play football that long. It's going to end sometime. I felt like I was good enough to keep playing. I knew I had to play my best so that nobody could come back on me and put a bad name on me for anything. I wanted my play to be so strong to where I wouldn't have to worry about some coaches coming back and messing things up.

I felt like he wanted to be so on point, by what happened at Notre Dame. I looked at him as a motivational speaker, and not a coach. There was to be no cursing, especially on the field. It was kind of funny and kind of weird.

Johnson: You've said before that the 2005 season was your best one from a personal standpoint.

Wallace: 2005 was my best year. I have to thank Willingham for that. He sat me down vs. Cal for the first quarter and I got a chip on my shoulder. It set me on fire and carried me through the year. He disciplined me for something that happened before [the season-opening game against] Air Force. I was doing my pre-game ritual and Willingham walked by and he saw me on my cell phone. Before every game I always talked to my Dad and my pastor, and I would pray. Willingham gave me a hard stare, and then for the next week's game against Cal I was benched for the first half.

Johnson: What did he say when he reprimanded you?

Wallace: He never said anything to me about why he was benching me. But the only thing it could have been was that cell phone incident. But it put a chip on my shoulder. I made 10 tackles in the second half against Cal.

Johnson: What was the overall environment like behind the scenes?

Wallace: It was the coaches versus the players. Willingham didn't make people feel like they could go to his office and talk to him. The coaches would go harder on us than what seemed like was right. We would wonder, do the coaches actually want us to succeed? I never had any bad personal experiences with Willingham because I would go out and play and he had to keep me on the field regardless of whether he liked me or not. I didn't care. As long as I made tackles on Saturday and my grades stayed up to par, I didn't care. A lot of guys suffered from the stifling environment because Tyrone had the close eye on them. He would use contacts to find out that you're hanging out with so-and-so. You'd ask him, "how do you know that?" He'd look straight at you and say, "I don't know."

We lost so many games. Even though he was making comments about needing to get the old guys out and get his guys in, we really wanted to win. But when one person stops believing, then one coach gets on him, then one coach gets on someone else, and suddenly you've got people losing faith because you've torn them down. Lots of guys were like that.

Johnson: Give a couple of examples.

Wallace: Guys like Corey Williams and Roy Lewis struggled to keep faith in themselves.

Johnson: That's especially interesting since Roy is now a defensive back with the Seahawks in the NFL. He also earned a Super Bowl ring while with the Pittsburgh Steelers in 2008. I heard through the grapevine that you helped convince Roy not to quit the team in 2007.

Wallace: Yeah, I had to talk to Roy because he wanted to stop playing football. He was going to be a firefighter. He was on track to graduate and was a good student. He had taken all his tests needed to become a firefighter. I had to talk to him, and beg him to reconsider. I was one year ahead of him and playing for the Seahawks. I told him, YOU CAN BE PLAYING AT THIS LEVEL! He didn't believe in himself. He felt like Willingham had taken all the life out of him. I kept telling him, "you're young, you're good. Trust me, you can play at this level. Just give it a go." Now he's been in the league for three years and he's loving it. I told him about all the good things and life in the NFL. You need to get here, this is where you need to be at. You've got God-given ability. Don't let yourself be stopped by Willingham, you're a baller.

You look at Steve Sarkisian and how he's doing things at Washington these days. Even though I don't see what's being done behind the scenes, when I watch them I can feel it. I don't sense favoritism, I just sense that it's fun.

Johnson: Fans and media, both locally and nationally, have long addressed Willingham as a man of great integrity and discipline. And yet there was this whole other reality going on behind the scenes. What is your take on that contrast between perception and reality?

Wallace: When they said a man of integrity, people were going off of how he looked and how he carried himself. And what he meant to do, and not the results. From his straight posture, to how correct he talked, and for what he accomplished in life, especially as an African-American. That was one of the things I loved about Coach Willingham. As an African-American, he's rubbed shoulders with a lot of powerful people and reached high levels. But integrity will only take you so far.

It felt like he tried to be perfect. As a black man I've never been in that position before. But he might have felt like he was carrying a burden. We would start a season like 1-2 and still be in the running, and then something goes wrong and Willingham suddenly starts throwing people under the bus. We would be like, dang, it's like that? In looking back after I graduated, I wondered if I should have spoken out.

Johnson: In looking back at your time playing under Willingham, what do you reflect on?

Wallace: After I graduated and it came time to spread my wings, I had no NFL Combine invite and I wasn't drafted. It was like how could that happen? To this day I don't know why. I was first team All Pac-10. I always felt like someone was putting a bad name on me. When it came time for the scouts, they would say they heard bad things about me, bad things about Dashon [Goldson], etc. Looking back, it felt like somebody screwed me. I was first team All Pac-10, and yet no Combine invite? I called them myself, asking why I didn't have an invite. They said no, you're not invited to be here.

Johnson: Why do you think that happened?

Wallace: I don't know. Everybody had their own beef with their position coaches because they were always getting chewed out, and Willingham always seemed like he was in the background. We got to thinking that maybe the coaches were doing things wrong, but in reality it was all coming from Willingham. But we didn't catch on for a while because Willingham was never around. That's how I came to my conclusion coming out of college and going to the NFL. The cover got pulled off my eyes. It was like maybe it was Willingham the whole time. A scout would say they heard such-and-such about so-and-so. And we would go talk to our position coaches and they would say they never told anyone that. And it only left one coach —Willingham.

Willingham took the good guy role, but maybe he knew what was going on the whole time. You know, if you've got a coach that you love, then you're going to respect him and you will want to play hard for him. Willingham didn't have anyone's respect. It was us versus him. Then the scouts come in, and Willingham never had anything good to say. I felt like he was speaking through his coaches and the coaches were doing his dirty work.

Johnson: Are there good traits about Willingham that are important to mention?

Wallace: Away from football, I think he's a great guy and a highly intelligent guy, especially as an African American, I always looked up to him. He changed my whole outlook on school. He showed me how hard it is being an African American man.

There was one time when I came back before spring break. Somebody back home had ended up [punching] me. I am in a meeting with my shades. Everyone is looking at me going what are you doing? Willingham orders me to take off my glasses. He sees the bruise on my face and says: "Put them back on. You're a great player so just make good decisions." To that point, I didn't see myself as a great player, so that made me believe in myself.

He was a good guy, so the whole thing was just kind of weird. We'll never know why.

Casey Paus had a tough day against Notre Dame in 2004

Offensive lineman Casey Bulyca loathed trainer Trent Greener

Defensive coordinator Kent Baer

Defensive lineman Manase Hopoi

Quarterback Johnny DuRocher

Safety C.J. Wallace gets helped off the turf following a knee injury

Johnie Kirton leaves the practice field

Returner/wide receiver Marlon Wood

Washington lines up against mighty Oklahoma

Linebacker E.J. Savannah

Offensive coordinator Tim Lappano, whose coaching was under fire from analyst Hugh Millen

Offensive lineman Stanley Daniels

Wide Receiver Marcel Reese caught a 98-yard touchdown pass from Jake Locker vs. Arizona in 2007

Louis Rankin: one of many undrafted Huskies who made NFL rosters

Washington quarterback Isaiah Stanback

CHAPTER 10

A Visit with Isaiah Stanback

Coming out of Seattle's Garfield High School, Isaiah Stanback was a prized member of Rick Neuheisel's final recruiting class at Washington. Heralded as the fifth-rated quarterback in the nation according to SuperPrep, Stanback was listed by numerous publications as one of the best recruits on the west coast.

After playing wide receiver during his redshirt freshman season of 2003, Stanback got his shot at quarterback in 2005 under new coach Tyrone Willingham. Stanback started all 11 games, throwing for 2,136 yards, scrambling for another 353 yards and scoring five touchdowns. In acknowledgement of his performance, Stanback was named Most Outstanding Offensive Player at the team's postseason banquet.

Stanback's mercurial career seemed destined for a sweet ending in his senior year of 2006, when the team forged a 4-1 start. But in an October game against Oregon State, he suffered a severe ankle injury that ended his collegiate career. Washington lost six of its final seven games and missed going to a bowl game with its 5-7 record.

Teammate's opinions of Stanback were largely favorable. Most viewed him as extremely likable and hard-working. Players like receiver Craig Chambers felt Stanback was a better quarterback than Jake Locker, and was overlooked partly because he was African-American. But others on the team questioned Stanback's mental toughness and composure during times of adversity. "He was Tyrone's guy though," said one player. "Players saw it, players knew."

Stanback was drafted in 2007 by the NFL's Dallas Cowboys. He currently plays wide receiver for the Seattle Seahawks.

Derek Johnson: When Tyrone Willingham came to Washington, the popular refrain in the media and among fans was that he was coming in to clean up a renegade program in disarray. What were your thoughts at the time about the big picture?

Isaiah Stanback: We were not a renegade program (chuckles). We went through some crap. A lot of the guys that came to Washington came there because of Rick Neuheisel. Most of the guys loved Neuheisel. I loved Neuheisel. He was, as they say, a player's coach, and we all looked forward to playing for him. Then he got set up by the NCAA and pushed out of there. Then Gilbertson was there for two years, and then Willingham came in 2005. I had three head coaches in five years. Continuity is important and we didn't have that. There's no free agency in college football so all the guys that came to play for Neuheisel didn't have many options. And when the next coach's style is completely different, it's so difficult. It's so incredibly difficult. And then a third guy comes in with yet another style. People on the outside don't understand just how tough that is for a football team.

Johnson: Soon after Willingham arrived, he demoted and then removed Steve Emtman from his position as strength coach. I've heard that you were passing a petition around the locker room in an effort to keep Emtman on the staff.

Stanback: Yes, I passed that around. I was happy that Steve was there; he was getting us tougher and stronger. He had been to the very top and knew what it took to become a champion. He was dedicated to teaching us how to get there too. It's not like he was there for the paycheck. When Willingham came in, before we knew what was happening, he took Steve away from us. It bothered me and I didn't understand it.

Johnson: I also heard that you didn't take kindly to having to cut your hair.

Stanback: It pissed me off. I understood what he was trying to do and I understood where coach Willingham was coming from. Eventually we became close. But the hair thing pissed me off because it had nothing to do with football, and I told him that. He felt that in the business world you can't have the long hair or be showing your tattoos. But with the Samoan and Tongan guys on the team, it wasn't just a hair style but it was part of their culture. Sometime it goes a lot deeper. And those guys were upset when they had to cut their hair. As for me, I had dreds. It takes a lot of work to create and maintain that, and I was made to cut it and it didn't make sense to me.

When Coach Willingham came in it was a rough start for a lot of guys. During that first press conference right, me and some of the other guys went up there to listen to him talk to the media. I don't even remember who all was with me. But I had two seasons left to play football so obviously a new coach coming in was a big deal for the rest of my career. After it was over, I tried to get out of there without being interviewed, but they got me cornered with the cameras rolling. It ended up on the news. Then I went over and met Coach Willingham for the first time. My first one-on-one with him, he chewed me out. He got on me for what I was wearing and for not being shaved. He wanted to know why I wasn't wearing a collared shirt. I was like, "what are you doing?" It rubbed me the wrong way. He told me that I always needed to be shaved and wear a collared shirt so that I would never be caught unprepared. That way if something came up I would be looking sharp and professional, and I would look like I knew what I was doing.

Over time I became pretty close with Coach Willingham. I had a different relationship with him than most of the guys on the team. I think a lot of it has to do with how you deal with his type of personality. He had that kind of military background. I understood where he was coming from because in high school I had a basketball coach who was like that. I didn't handle it as well back then but I had learned from it.

Willingham's strict way of doing things rubbed guys the wrong way. But it's in how you deal with it that makes the difference. A lot of guys would walk away pissed off without saying something and allow for a misunderstanding to exist. On the other hand, I would always want to know why. I would always ask questions to find out why they wanted something done a certain way.

Johnson: That's interesting to hear because several of your teammates told me that Scott White was always asking coaches why they were doing things a certain way. It sounds like that's what sent him straight into Willingham's doghouse. Guys have told me that it was critical to be a "yes sir, no sir" kind of guy to get playing time. And yet you're saying that you constantly asked why, and it seems like it didn't cause the same problems for you. What was the difference?

Stanback: Well there are certain ways of asking things. It's like when you get pulled over by the police. You can be rude or you can be respectful. But I'm definitely not a "yes sir, no sir" kind of guy. I was raised by my mom to always ask questions and not just accept things on the surface because someone told me it's a certain way. But if someone is chewing you out or is looking to provoke a reaction from you, a lot of guys on the team took the initial [defensive] reaction instead of holding back. They don't think about the backlash they're going to get. When you react on the streets to someone trying to provoke you then you'll get cleaned out. Like I would tell [UW defensive back] Vonzell McDowell that sometimes you have to swallow your words. You can't appear to be telling a coach off. If you're out of position or the coach isn't doing things the way you think he should, you can't react in a way that can be perceived as disrespectful. A lot of times in football, and in life in general, it's a political game and you have to play it right or you're going to pay the price. The coaches hold all the power and they have you by the balls.

A lot of guys came from different backgrounds, coming from the inner city and the streets. Their first reaction is to get defensive. I loved Scott White to death. But Scott came from the streets of San Diego, and he had a temper. Me and him always needed to have the last word. But he didn't have that switch to shut off his mouth like I had. I would just shut my mouth. He would keep talking and wear you down and wait you out and then get in the final word. That's how he is and that's what killed Scott.

If you're going to talk to a coach that makes them feel like their competence is being questioned in front of everybody, then you're going to get screwed. I know that from experience, because I got screwed in the Gilbertson era.

Johnson: Go into that a bit.

Stanback: They were very upset that I refused to switch to wide receiver. I had been recruited as a quarterback. During the 2004 season, they had me third string behind Casey Paus and Carl Bonnell. The coaches were calling me out all the time for being selfish.

Johnson: Calling you selfish to your face?

Stanback: Oh yeah. Several times I would be in stretch lines and they would walk past and say "you're so selfish for not switching to wide receiver." But I never saw them asking [quarterbacks] Casey Paus or Carl Bonnell to switch to wide receiver. They set me up to fail. When we went to Notre Dame in 2004, I was third string, and the very next week we traveled to Los Angeles to play [top-ranked] USC, and they made me the starter for that game. We only ran 14 plays out of 150 plays on the play sheet. We lost bad [38-0]. They set me up to fail.

There were so many times I wanted to explode. So many times that I wanted to rip into the coaches and let them know how pissed off I was. It got so bad that I wasn't talking to anybody. I wasn't having any part of it. I would go to practice and then go to the locker room and then go home. I'm not the transferring kind of guy, but the thought crossed my mind. There were guys in the media that knew I was being screwed by Gilbertson. They would ask me questions and try to get me to talk about it. I didn't say much of anything. I knew I was in a no-win situation. Everyone knew I should have been playing.

Johnson: Off the top of my head I do remember the 2004 Apple Cup in Pullman, which was Gilbertson's last game as head coach. The Cougars hadn't won an Apple Cup in seven years. UW was down something like 28-9, and then you were put in and the Huskies rallied but fell short 28-25. I was wondering why you hadn't been put in earlier.

Stanback: Yeah, I sat for the entire first half freezing my butt off (laughs). I think Casey Paus threw four interceptions in the first half. The last one bounced off Tusi Sa'au's helmet. Gilbertson finally said to me: "You're going in." We scored some points in the second half but did fall short. That was another time where I was just thrown into the fire. I felt like I was going to explode with frustration.

Johnson: And you sought out former Husky Warren Moon.

Stanback: I got hooked up with Warren Moon, because what he went through was far worse than what I was going through. He took me out. We went and grabbed something to eat. He told me to just keep my head up and keep grinding. He said that they may have the title of coach but at the end of the day they're human beings just like me. They just have the title of coach and have all the power that comes with it. He said just keep grinding and be ready for when your time finally comes.

Johnson: But you came to see the coaches as having all the power.

Stanback: Absolutely. When a coach gets mad at you, he'll screw you. He will tell scouts bad things about you; he has all the power. Scouts can't talk to us players; their information can only come from the coaches. So if a coach wants to make you look bad he will. That's how it's played. It had an effect on a lot of guys, and had an effect on my career.

That was what I loved about Coach Willingham when he arrived. He made it clear that nobody was safe. Me, Carl and Casey would all compete for the starting job. It would be fair and even competition. I loved that I was getting a fair shot to be the quarterback. I had nothing but total respect for my position coaches, particularly [offensive coordinator] Tim Lappano. When they came in, I talked with Lappano and told him that I was willing to work hard and do whatever was necessary to become the best quarterback I could be. I had a great relationship with him and have nothing but the greatest respect for him.

Johnson: Former Husky Jamal Fountaine said that Willingham had the right message for the players, especially the black players, but he had no idea how to communicate that message to them. He was also critical of Willingham's staff. He said that Neuheisel's staff was composed of good teachers, but that he didn't see much teaching going on from Willingham's staff. In particular, he said that Kent Baer was an "asshole" and made things way too complicated for the players.

Stanback: I don't know if I can speak about Coach Baer, because he was coaching defense and we were usually separated on different sides of the field. I talked to Coach Baer from time-to-time, and I thought he was cool. I know A LOT of guys on the team didn't like him at all. I talked with him and joked around with him. But lots of guys on the team couldn't stand him. The coach I knew best was Tim Lappano. He reminded me of my mom, in that he never said anything to me just to make me feel better. He had coached in the NFL and it was a cut throat NFL way of teaching that he gave us. I liked his style. He was hard on me, but he made me a better person and a better quarterback.

Johnson: After your career was over and you were in the NFL, public criticism of Tyrone Willingham grew. You spoke up in the media as a show of support for him.

Stanback: Yes, I did. First and foremost I did it for the sake of stability for the program, and especially for Jake [Locker]. I had gone through three different coaching staffs and went through so much crap. I didn't want Jake to have to go through that. I didn't want any of the guys to go through that again.

Linebacker Scott White reflects on his career while cradling the 2006 Apple Cup trophy

CHAPTER 11

White Was Seeing Red

"Success is never final, failure is never fatal. It's courage that counts."
—John Wooden, legendary UCLA basketball coach

BEING quotable may not have endeared linebacker Scott White to his coaches, but during the miserable 2004 season, White became a beacon to sportswriters looking for entertaining copy as the losses and repetitive gloomy quotes from teammates accumulated.

Bob Condotta of *The Seattle Times* saw it that year when he asked White about his post-college plans. The young linebacker paused, smiled and then said: "I'd like to have your job, man, to be honest with you." Condotta had fun with that one, writing the next day: "... That was, apparently, the first time in recent memory that a Husky professed a desire to see things from the ink-stained wretch's point of view."

White wasn't only outspoken, he was also a good player. "Scott White, he was my boy," said safety C.J. Wallace. "Scott was a great linebacker, very quick to the ball, and probably the most intelligent football player I've ever been around."

Stanley Daniels of the Denver Broncos laughed when thinking back to his UW days. "Coaches didn't like him because he would tell you how he feels," Daniels said. "Me, if I had an issue to discuss, I would go and talk to a coach one-on-one in private. But Scott would tell you how he feels right on the spot. Everyone who knows him knows that. And I love him for it. We all did. Coaches didn't like it though."

White came from San Diego where he starred at Mission Bay High School. The San Diego Union-Tribune named him San Diego's

Defensive Player of the Year for 2001. The scholarship offers flooded in from numerous schools, including the big boys of college football: USC, LSU, Nebraska, and the Oklahoma Sooners, who flew him to the Midwest in a private plane. But White had been in Seattle to see the Huskies beat the USC Trojans, and he wanted to play for Rick Neuheisel. White's brothers thought he was insane to not go to one of the monster schools, but during his freshman year White vowed: "We are going to win something here. ... One day we are going to win the Rose Bowl. Mark it down. You see how the young players are playing right now. Eventually we will be the veterans."

By his junior season in 2005, White started every game at linebacker and ranked fourth in tackles with 79. On national TV against Notre Dame he recorded 10 tackles, two for a loss, and one sack. Blaine Newnham of *The Seattle Times* referred to him as "a terror off the edge." White found Willingham odd and overbearing that first year, but conflict wouldn't manifest between the two until winter conditioning drills in early 2006.

While participating in a drill overseen by assistant coach Eric Yarber, White pulled a hamstring. "The coaches felt like I was faking," White recalled. "Everybody that knows anything about sports medicine knows that if there's bruising or discoloration on any muscle, you've got problems."

As White rehabbed and C.J. Wallace recovered from shoulder surgery, the two would run around the field but not take part in drills. They went past Mike Denbrock's station, and the coach shouted: "There's two of our best players taking the day off! You guys are faking! You're just trying to get out of real work!" Wallace didn't respond while White laughed in an attempt to show he wasn't bothered, even though he was. Later that week, as White sat on the training table, cornerback Dashon Goldson looked at him and said, "Damn, both of your hamstrings are messed up?" Ugly discoloration had appeared on both legs.

Come Spring Ball 2006, White endured more pain than ever. "I'm out there participating, but I'm hurt," White said. "That was my thing, running around making plays, but I couldn't run. But the coaches said I was faking, so I was out there practicing. They were grading me as if I was healthy. They were telling me how terrible I was doing. For them to have me out there running around was insanity, but they were trying to use me to motivate the team. I'm running with the twos but I'm not trippin' because the season is months away."

The months passed quickly and suddenly the first day of fall camp was underway at Husky Stadium. By this time, media wasn't allowed to view anything other than the stretching exercises. Bob Condotta of *The Seattle Times* spotted White lining up with the second team and not with the starters. Later when he had the chance, Condotta cornered the linebacker.

In an August 10th article entitled *Demotion at Linebacker Has White Seeing Red*, Condotta cited the 20 games that White had started since his sophomore season, which was second most on the team. Condotta described Scott White's surprise demotion in favor of junior Dan Howell. Howell, a well-liked youngster, was universally considered a great teammate, but a vastly inferior athlete compared to White. White didn't hide his hurt. "Having my degree already kind of gives me a little more contentment with the whole situation [and] having the ability to walk away from it all," he said. "I'm not saying that's what I want to do, but it's about buying in, and if it's a role that I can't accept, I'm not going to be a burden on this football team. I'm not going to be a distraction. So if that's the role and I'm not happy with that role, that's something I may consider."

The statement enraged Willingham when it surfaced in the next day's newspaper. He summoned White into his office and ripped into him. Looking across the desk, Willingham's imposing glare bore down on the senior linebacker. He asked White why he said those things.

"I understand why you're upset, but I answered the questions honestly," White replied.

"You have embarrassed me and this football team."

"Why are you doing this?"

"Because you're in a position battle."

"What is the position battle about? Is this a real competition or is this something you're creating?"

Willingham outlined his reasons why Howell deserved to start over White.

"Coach Willingham, are you watching the same tape I am?" asked White. "What are you seeing?"

When Coach Willingham stared back and said nothing, White rose from his seat. "I can't play for you anymore."

"That's fine," said Willingham. "I will give you your release and you are free to leave this team."

By the time White got back home, his phone was ringing off the hook as teammates tracked him down. Stanley Daniels, Isaiah Stanback, Mark Palaita and Kenny James were all right in his face telling him he couldn't leave. White felt the ambivalence that Casey Paus had experienced when considering leaving his teammates.

After expending much effort persuading White to return, Stanley Daniels went to the Connibear Shellhouse for a private meeting with his head coach. "I told Willingham that he couldn't do this," recalled Daniels. "I told him I didn't understand why, and I didn't understand what was going on. I said: 'Scott's a team leader and his teammates love him. Right now he's acting with emotion. But he made a mistake. We need him.'"

According to Daniels, Willingham said they were doing it to see how White would respond. "You're doing *what*?" asked Daniels in disbelief. "We're seniors, okay? Scott was second team all Pac-10 last year. He's probably our best linebacker. What do you mean you want to see how he'll respond? What are you thinking?"

The media was equally confused by Willingham's rationale. "I always say that everything is up in the air, it doesn't matter who you are," he told reporters. "I think Isaiah Stanback is our starting quarterback. But if his performance doesn't dictate that, then the next guy, if he's playing well, gets the opportunity. And I think our guys are starting to understand if you are an All-American, you should perform and practice at an All-American level. If you are not and then the next guy comes on, then you are not an All-American anymore."

Later that day, White conceded to his teammates that they were right. He swallowed his pride and returned to Willingham's office. The coach was willing to listen, but held off on starting the meeting until assistant coaches Kent Baer and Chris Tormey could be brought in and witness the repentance. "I want to be part of this team and I made a mistake," White said to the three coaches.

Willingham relented and White was back. But, as Willingham made clear, he was demoting White to the scout team. He would need to work his way back up. White was fine with that. Later that day, over near the old media room in the corner of Hec Ed Pavilion, White had an hour long heart-to-heart talk with Baer.

"You're dumber than I thought you were," Baer said. "You can't understand what we're trying to do here? We're just sending a message. We were trying to use you as an example to the whole team."

Baer explained how he had gone to Willingham and told him that he needed White back on the team. "Scottie, I am on your side, I am in your corner," Baer said.

"That meant a lot to me," White recalled years later. "He was trying to do what was right."

The players were joyous to have White back. "Don't even trip, we knows its bullshit," Stanback said to him.

"All the players were telling me that," said White. "In the locker room, everybody knew."

Outside the locker room was another story. The radio airwaves were filled with people calling White a quitter and saying the team was better off without him. On the heavily-trafficked message boards of Dawgman.com, countless posts stated how Willingham was clearing the cancer out of the team in order to rebuild it back to its former glory. White heard and read a lot of comments, and they stung him.

"Public fallout was tough," he said. "People were saying ugly things about me, but my hands were tied. I was being too perceptive, listening to things everyone was saying about me, character assassinations and attacks. It affected me, it got me down."

White bore down for the rest of camp. Every day, he wrote SHOW THEM on his left wrist tape. He dominated drill after drill, and right before the season opener against San Jose State, he was the first-stringer at WIL linebacker.

White played with hamstring pain the entire season. But he had his most productive year. "It was largely due to the position change to WIL linebacker where I could be more active and make plays," he said.

The 2006 season ended with the 35-32 win over the Cougars, which snapped the annual six game losing streak. Just like that, White's collegiate career was over. He thought the chance for the NFL was there, but interest in him seemed almost non-existent.

"I heard from my agent that the word was out that I had character issues and wasn't getting along with people and was a quitter," White said. "An agent told me that our coaching staff wasn't very high on this group of seniors. He said they are putting out the word to basically stay away from these guys."

These days White is coaching linebackers at Palomar College in Southern California. "I know in my heart and being around football long enough, I know I could have played in the NFL, at least as a free agent," White says. "C.J. and Isaiah told me that I was good enough to play at that level. That was my consolation. The spin at Washington under Willingham was always to say that we didn't have a lot of talent. But how many guys did we have that were signed as unrestricted free agents and then stick with teams? If it's so hard to do, the most difficult thing to do, why were the Washington guys the ones doing that? How could Roy Lewis , C.J. Wallace, Louis Rankin, Marcel Reece and others not get drafted and then make 53-man rosters? The talent was there if not the depth. You saw it so many times after games when coaches threw the players under the bus. To me that was the biggest problem with Coach Willingham. There was always an excuse, but no accountability. He sat there in meetings always talking about accountability, but when push came to shove, he never took accountability."

W

Safety Chris Hemphill playing in the
Los Angeles Coliseum as a freshman in 2004

CHAPTER 12

Suddenly Senior

"When you think about incredibly talented people like Chris Hemphill, what would have happened if he had been given his senior year? You could be possibly destroying this person's dreams. You're denying him an opportunity plus you're hurting his reputation."

—C.J. Wallace, former UW safety

BY 2006, Husky football players all knew the deal: If you enter Willingham's doghouse, you're *never* coming out. Somewhere along the line safety Chris Hemphill found his way into the doghouse. At 6'5" and 235 pounds, Hemphill was rangy, fast, and capable of ferocious hitting. Teammates often told the story from fall camp when heralded 280 pound tailback Johnie Kirton first came to Washington in 2004. To see Kirton line up in the backfield startled observers not prepared for it. On this particular day in August, Kirton took a handoff and ran like a steamroller off right tackle. Hemphill, just a redshirt freshman, came flying in from his free safety position like a kamikaze pilot and battered Kirton with a bone crushing hit. Kirton crumpled to the turf as someone on defense towered over him and shouted "Welcome to Washington!" Teammates mobbed Hemphill. They all knew he could play.

Hemphill's freshman season of 2004 seemed to portend great things to come. He played in eight games both on defense and special teams. Off-the-field, he sported a 3.5 GPA and was named an honorable mention selection to the Pac-10's All-Academic Team.

But when Willingham arrived in 2005, something about Hemphill displeased the new coach. Hemphill saw limited duty all season long, almost all of it on special teams. It carried into the first five games of 2006. Teammates all wondered what the deal was. Hemphill worked hard, was well liked by his teammates, and was deemed one of the top athletes on the team. And yet he sat.

"We had no problems on that team," recalled strong safety C.J. Wallace. "We didn't have the kind of team where guys got into trouble. There was something about Chris that Coach [Willingham] didn't like about him and kept him off the field. I always felt like he should have been on the field. I felt like the perfect lineup in the backfield would have been me and Chris at the safety positions, and Dashon Goldson and Roy Lewis at the corners. Me, Dashon and Roy all made it to the NFL. We would have had the best secondary in the nation, and the best safety tandem in the nation with me and Chris. It wasn't hard to see, and I couldn't understand why Willingham couldn't see it.

"Chris had to play that much better than everybody else. He had to go balls out. Because if it was even close, he wasn't going to play. He had to be so much better than everyone else so there would be no comparison. [Secondary] Coach J.D. Williams would get on him a lot because he wanted Chris to play and he didn't feel like Chris was taking things seriously enough in practice. But Chris is so tall and so big he looks like he's coasting through things. So Willingham thought he never played hard and was too nonchalant. I went to Coach J.D. plenty of times and told him I wanted Chris in the backfield with me; I wanted Chris at safety with me. I knew what he could do. We were waiting for him to get his chance to play, we knew that he could play."

To this day, Chris Hemphill doesn't know why Willingham soured on him. But he does know the moment that sealed his fate, when he entered the doghouse foursquare. It was the week Washington prepared to travel to Los Angeles to take on powerhouse USC. During practice, UW receiver Marcel Reece ran a crossing route and caught the football. Coach Williams had been preaching the need to strip the ball to the defensive backs. Hemphill ran up and tried to rip the ball from Reece's grasp, but their feet got tangled and Hemphill fell to the turf while Reece broke free and ran up field. Williams shouted and berated Hemphill for the gaffe.

As Hemphill got to his feet and returned to the huddle, he retorted: "I'm trying to do what you said! Fuck!"

J.D Williams became infuriated. "Hemphill, get the fuck off the field!"

Hemphill went over to the sideline as practice continued. From a distance he watched as Willingham and Williams converged for several minutes, pointing toward him and talking. Suddenly his name was off all special teams, and he was cut from the traveling squad for the USC game.

"USC was near my home," said Hemphill. "Willingham didn't have me on the travel schedule. I apologized to Coach Williams, and then I went to Coach Willingham and apologized. I told him that I had been doing everything he wanted me to do. He said: 'You have an attitude that is detrimental to this team. You are not going to be traveling with the team to Los Angeles.'"

Dozens of Hemphill's teammates recalled that one day in practice as the only time Hemphill ever cursed at a coach. He had been no trouble off the field and was a good student. He had even recorded a rap CD with several teammates for a Seattle-based nonprofit organization that provides free, professional photography for children facing life-threatening illnesses.

But when Washington traveled to the Los Angeles Coliseum to take on the Trojans, Hemphill was back in Seattle watching on TV. "Family and friends were calling saying 'we don't see you, is everything all right?' They were looking for me, and it kind of hurt, because I wasn't even there. My DB coach knew I should have been out there, but it was Willingham's call. I was starting to feel like the end for me might be coming soon."

Willingham was making periodic comments to the team that he needed to start getting rid of some guys and bring in his kind of recruits. When it came to Hemphill, many players wondered amongst themselves why Jason Wells was continuing to start at free safety even though everyone agreed he wasn't anywhere near as talented as Hemphill. The reason was that Wells possessed the kind of absolute compliance Willingham sought. "Chris had his own kind of swag," said a teammate. "Willingham didn't like that. But I would have given the shirt off my back for Chris. We all would have. He was a great guy, a great teammate."

"Hearing Willingham say that they needed to get rid of guys and make room for their recruits, it sucked to hear that from our own coach," Hemphill said. "Maybe he said that out of frustration because we were losing so much. But the coaches got to be accountable too. If you're going throw the players under the bus, throw yourself under there too."

In the ninth game of the year, Washington was playing Arizona State at Husky Stadium. The Huskies were in the midst of their annual six game losing streak. Jason Wells went down with a concussion and Hemphill took his place. His performance was so-so. He remembered a missed tackle of Sun Devil running back Ryan Terrain. "I went to wrap him up and I bounced off him," Hemphill said. "Coach Willingham let me know about it. Later on I was on the punt return team. A gunner's job was to double team the guy running down the field. As he's approaching I hear Willingham shout 'get him Chris, get him!' I blocked the guy, but he falls off me. Right when our punt returner gets the ball, the tackler split between me and a teammate and made the tackle. I heard Coach yell 'C'mon! You gotta make that block!'"

The following Tuesday, as the Huskies prepared to travel to Eugene to play Oregon, Willingham called Hemphill into his office.

"Chris, I've been thinking about this, and I have chosen not to renew your scholarship for next year," Willingham said coldly.

"Wow Coach, I can't believe this. Why are you doing this?"

"Your attitude is a detriment to this football team and I don't want you on this team anymore."

"I thought I had done everything you asked me to do. I've worked hard. I can't believe this is happening."

"When we play Stanford in a week and a half, it will be the final home game of the year. You will be joining the seniors as they are introduced before the ball game."

"Even though I'm a junior?"

"You are a senior now," said Willingham. "You're on track to getting your degree and you will move on from here."

The conversation was coming to an end, but Willingham had one more item to discuss.

"Chris, as you know, Jason Wells is injured so you will be starting this week at Oregon. Chris, I need for you to ball for me this week. I need you to perform."

Hemphill left the office feeling like his spirit was crushed. There was still practice that day, so he went straight to the empty locker room and slumped upon a bench staring at the floor. "Guys were filtering into the locker room," Hemphill said. "I sat at my locker and thought about what he said and what I was going to do next. I was on track to graduate, that was all I knew. It was hard to put my pads on that day."

Hemphill wasn't alone in receiving bad news. Three other juniors were told they were suddenly seniors. They were defensive back Durrell Moss, wide receiver/kick returner Marlon Wood and place-kicker Michael Braunstein. Durrell Moss's heart was no longer in it and the Washington athletic department suddenly realized that Wood's eligibility had expired from a year he had spent at Alabama State in 2003, even though he hadn't played football. Placekicker Michael Braunstein was infuriated and went to athletic director Todd Turner to complain. What was baffling in Braunstein's case was that Willingham had written him a glowing letter of recommendation not even two weeks prior.

"Todd Turner said that this was Tyrone Willingham's team," recalled Braunstein. "He told me that the athletic department had no say in what happens within the football team. He said he had no control and couldn't do anything for me. So I went back to Willingham. He told me I would be introduced with the seniors for the Stanford game. I told him that I wouldn't do that. I didn't understand why he was doing this. I was credited on their website for doing community service, I was good on the field, I had made 8 field goals in a row at that point, I had a 3.2 GPA and I was the only football player in the Business School. So I was doing things the right way. I demanded to know why. He said I wasn't getting along with the trainer and that others were going to see me behaving that way and it sets a bad example. He told me: 'You're a detriment to this football team and you're out of here.'"

When Washington arrived that Saturday at Autzen Stadium to play the heavily-favored Ducks, Chris Hemphill got dressed while exhibiting a subdued demeanor. His teammate and cousin Roy Lewis came up to him for a heart-to-heart.

"How ya doing cuz?"

"You know how I'm doing."

"I know how you're feeling. All the guys know what's going on and they know its bullshit. But we need you to put it aside."

"It's too damn hard."

"We need you today. Forget the coaches. Fuck them. Your teammates need you. It's a T.V. game. This is your chance to go out there and show them what you're about."

"Okay… you're right," Hemphill replied, looking directly at Lewis.

The Huskies in their traveling whites poured out from the tunnel and took their place on the visitor's sideline while the Duck faithful booed their presence lustily. Oregon was heavily favored and few thought Washington stood much of a chance. But as Chris Hemphill took to the field in making his first start as a Husky, he felt at home. On the first play from scrimmage, Oregon ran a reverse. Hemphill sniffed it out and made the tackle.

"I went out there and just felt like I was where I belonged in the first place," Hemphill said. "I was out there with Roy, Dashon and C.J. next to me at safety. It was where I was supposed to be. So I just did what I do, which is play football. I ended up making 14 tackles with a fumble recovery and an interception. And the interception would have been a touchdown if Scott White would have blocked Dennis Dixon," he added with a chuckle.

On one occasion, as Hemphill returned to the sideline, Willingham patted him on the helmet and said "keep it up." At another part of the game, teammate Desmond Davis leaned into Hemphill's ear. "Hey bro, you should have heard coach J.D., when you made that interception. He was jumping up and down shoutin' 'I knew that guy was a player! I knew it!"

As the game drew to a close, Oregon crushed Washington as expected by a twenty-point margin. Their vaunted running back Jonathan Stewart racked up 159 yards and two touchdowns. That hurt doubly for Husky fans, since Stewart was a state of Washington product that Oregon had lured away from Seattle. Stewart had confided in former Husky legend Ron Holmes that Willingham made little effort to recruit him.

But the topic that intrigued the media and had people talking was Chris Hemphill. He had been all over the field. In fact, someone with a microphone swooped in as soon as the clock hit 0:00.

"A media guy grabbed me to do an interview on about the 30-yard line," Hemphill said. "I talked to him for a minute before Coach [Bob] Simmons shouted at me. He yelled 'Hemp! Get your ass over here! You end that interview right now!' I told the interviewer that I couldn't talk right then. I started heading toward the tunnel which was behind the end zone. Willingham was staring at me the entire time I was walking back. Hand over his mouth. Our eyes were locked for several moments.

"There was no rule in the handbook about no interviews after the game. But Willingham did not like that. So we got to the locker room and guys get dressed. Then the media wanted to talk to me. Many of them are saying: 'This is the best game of your career. Who are you? Where have you been? Why have you been hiding?'

"I could have easily bad mouthed him, but I said Willingham is a great coach and a great guy. I said that if he feels it's not best for the team for me to be out there, then I'm going to respect that decision. I knew that bad mouthing him wouldn't help me. And I told them I would only answer questions about the game after that."

The Tuesday following the Oregon game, Willingham summoned Hemphill to his office. The young man harbored a fleeting hope that his coach had changed his mind, but Willingham simply congratulated him on a good performance and told him he was starting again versus Stanford. Willingham then reiterated that Hemphill would join the seniors when they were introduced that Saturday. And just like that, the meeting was over. Hemphill's career at Washington, along with that of his three "Suddenly Senior" teammates, was coming to a truncated conclusion.

"Hemphill was so talented," said former teammate and offensive lineman Stanley Daniels, now with the NFL's Denver Broncos. "The kid goes out there against Oregon and has a monster game. He was a great teammate and a great guy. He was 6'5" 230 pounds and was ballin'. Willingham takes away his scholarship because he didn't like him. We were so upset at Willingham. When we signed with Coach Neuheisel back in 2003 he promised us we would have five years to try to win a national championship and further ourselves as players. He told me that in my living room. But Willingham comes in and takes away the fifth year of several players. You don't take away a kid's fifth year just because you don't like him. You can't expect the remaining players to be okay with that. I will never be okay with that. And it's hard for me as a black man to say that because I am a Willingham supporter."

As the team prepared for Stanford, the plight of Hemphill, Braunstein, Moss and Wood became a media controversy in Seattle. Paul Braunstein, Michael's father, sent out a press release to media outlets to raise awareness. Articles emerged in newspapers and the topic became a hot one on local sports radio and on message boards like Dawgman.com. As Willingham met with the media that week, he was clearly perturbed by the criticism. When a reporter asked him why Chris Hemphill was being cut from the team considering his performance at Oregon, Willingham said: "Chris knows why I made the decision." When asked about several current Huskies joining a Facebook group called "I Support Braunstein and Hemphill," Willingham snapped: "Don't go there."

"If my timing was off in delivering those announcements, it was only because I want them to have all the things that they should have," Willingham said. "I don't think you deprive a young man of an opportunity to walk on the field for the last time. If that was my mistake, I apologize, but I don't ever want to be dishonest with our young men."

Willingham ordered his players to not discuss the situation with the media, but they were collectively furious. "This guy was ruining a lot of college guy's lives and careers based on a personal vendetta," said a former Husky now in the NFL. "If he had a personal vendetta against you, if you didn't show up for a class or he thought you looked at him cross-eyed, you were going into the doghouse. And if you went into the doghouse, you wouldn't ever get out. He wouldn't give you an explanation, and even if you were the best player on the team, you would never play again in the purple and gold."

The public outcry led the media to contact athletic director Todd Turner that Friday. He gave Willingham his full support. "The coach has the discretion about membership on his team and we don't interfere with that at all," Turner said. "We want to make sure that proper policies and rules are followed, but the coach determines who is on the squad and who plays, not the athletic administration."

Aside from all the dire drama, there was still a game to play, and the Huskies still had a chance to go to a bowl game. While they had lost five straight games and possessed a 4-6 record, they only needed a 6-6 record to go bowling. The remaining games against Stanford and Washington State were absolutely winnable. Stanford in particular, under floundering coach Walt Harris, was college football's worst that season. They arrived in Seattle with a 0-10 record. Their rush defense was the worst in the nation, surrendering nearly six yards per carry. On the Husky pre-game radio show on KJR, football analyst Hugh Millen predicted the Husky running game was about to have a big day.

But in the Washington locker room, as players got ready for the game, the mournful mood extended to every member of the team. "Guys were crying," said a former player. "I was telling the guys that we need to pull this thing together or we're going to get our asses kicked. Guys just didn't want to play. It was a shitty deal. That kind of thing should never happen to a college athlete."

On top of the foul mood, some players considered the downside of beating Stanford. Many expressed a desire to lose one of the games to avoid having to go to a bowl game, due to the additional three weeks of practice they would have to endure under Willingham.

"That situation just destroyed that locker room," said an anonymous member of the UW staff. "They were all caught off guard. They were shattered. Other guys were asking what does that mean for them in the future? The ramifications for recruiting were tough. Our rivals could point to us and say if you go to Washington there's no guarantee you're going to be given your full five years."

As the somber Huskies filed into the team room for their pre-game position meetings, there were photos on the wall that Willingham put up. They were photos of hotels and attractions from possible bowl destinations, should the Huskies win out. Nobody cared as everyone's mind was on the Suddenly Senior situation. "We didn't hear it from Willingham," said a former player. "He never said anything to the team about what he did to Chris, Mike, Marlon and Durrell. He never addressed it. It all came straight from the players themselves."

The seniors were introduced, one-by-one, to the Husky Stadium crowd. True to his defiant vow, Michael Braunstein refused to take part. The game started. Washington went through the motions and Johnny DuRocher, making a rare start, was knocked out of the game with a concussion. Even though the Huskies entered halftime knotted at 3-3, things inevitably slipped away from them in the second half. Washington's quarterbacks were a combined 11-of-44 passing. The UW running game mustered a paltry 39 yards on 28 carries. By the end, the Stanford Cardinal, owners of a 0-10 record, got their only win in 2006, beating Washington 20-3. It was Stanford's first win in Husky Stadium in thirty years.

"I went out there and did what I was supposed to," Hemphill said. "I played my heart out the same even though I hurt my hamstring. As the game went on I felt it getting worse." Early in the fourth quarter, Hemphill chased Stanford's Richard Sherman down the sideline on a 74-yard touchdown reception. "I could tell if I kept running the thing was going to snap. But when coaches saw it on film, they thought I was loafing. I still led the team in tackles again, 10 tackles. But I knew my time was running out."

The loss left the Huskies at 4-7 and knocked them out of bowl eligibility. All that remained was a game at Washington State in Pullman. "They told me that Jason Wells was starting," said Hemphill. "It was my last game as a Husky. It was a giant slap in my face."

But the players talked amongst themselves all week and made a pact. To hell with the coaches was their thought—this one's for us and the seniors.

The Huskies came out into the outdoor meat locker that is Martin Stadium in November. Running back Louis Rankin ripped off a 77-yard touchdown run. Quarterback Carl Bonnell connected with Cody Ellis and Marcel Reece for a pair of long touchdown passes. Reserve linebacker Chris Stevens blocked a Cougar punt and recovered it for a touchdown. Backup linebacker Caesar Rayford begged and pleaded to be put into the game, and sacked WSU's Alex Brink at the end of the game—Rayford's only tackle all season. The final score: Washington 35, Washington State 32.

In the aftermath, Chris Hemphill felt bittersweet emotions. "I kept telling coach I was ready I want to play," he said. "I was happy that we won and I cheered on my teammates, but it hurt to barely get out there. It was my last game, and I had nothing to show for it."

The scene in the visitor's locker room was sheer bedlam. The Huskies screamed, hollered, cried, embraced, shouted and danced.

"That game was great," recalled C.J. Wallace. "Just playing that game and winning that game, I felt like I closed the chapter to my college career. Even though I never went to a bowl game, it made me feel glad that I was a Husky and made me feel glad that I went to Washington. I feel like the team did something for me and did something for the seniors. Everybody fought. I tore my meniscus and I had to play because there was no choice. I played with my knee torn. It was the first time the offense and defense clicked at the same time. It was the best gift. Chris Stevens had the blocked punt for a touchdown. I had never seen Cody [Ellis] score before. I rarely saw him get a pass. But Cody did his thing, man. Everybody got a chance to play. In the locker room, we were celebrating after the game. The seniors said some words. I usually wasn't vocal, but I said a few words. I remember our defensive coordinator Kent Baer, who everybody hated because he was the meanest guy. He came up to me and said he was proud of me. Up to that point, we had always bumped heads and I thought he hated me. Then I thought, well maybe it wasn't him, maybe like everything else it went back to Willingham."

It was a noticeably lighter-hearted Tyrone Willingham that faced reporters. He made a couple dry quips. Then he said: ""I just think it speaks to the courage of our young men. I'm proud of them for doing that... Even though this has been a rough ride the last five or six weeks, I have enjoyed this season. I can see the growth in this football team, even when others can't."

Blaine Newnham of *The Seattle Times* took stock the next day of the Suddenly Senior situation and the team as a whole. Newnham wrote: "There was an irony that Willingham, who champions the cause of players and whose ethics have never been questioned, allowed himself to become the coach who would dump a player just to gain a scholarship. Willingham drew the criticism upon himself and his program, when in an attempt to be decent, he informed the players that they were not coming back so they could enjoy the normal senior activities. He could have quietly purged them in the spring. In college coaching, Willingham is the steak, rather than the sizzle. He doesn't make noise, but he does care for and graduates kids. He demands accountability, and toughness."

With the season concluded, Chris Hemphill now assessed his future. After talking it over with his parents, he transferred to Central Washington University. "We ended up having one of the best seasons in school history," he said. "My friend Chris Rohrbach was there; he transferred there the year before. And he said, 'Come down here and bring Charles [Smith] and Durrell with you and let's go win a championship.' I laughed at first, and I was in talks with Nevada-Las Vegas to be a cornerback. But then they changed the transfer rules that you had to be graduated already, but I was still about twenty credits short. So now I could only go to a Division II school.

"So I went to Central," Hemphill continued. "Ended up an All-American. Led the conference in interceptions. We took the team to the third round of the playoffs. It was liberating. The coaches believed in me. Even though it was my first year, I was basically in charge of the defense, and I got to use my experience. I felt at home, they welcomed me there. They made sure I was happy with my classes. I found a place to live close to the university. It was a small college town atmosphere. We were winning, which I wasn't used to. It was a breath of fresh air.

"After that season was over, I was talking to my agent Chris Cates. He said he didn't know where we were going to do my pro day. He said there was bad blood at Washington. He talked to Willingham, they agreed to allow me but I had to talk to them first. I flew to Seattle and met with [offensive line] coach [Mike] Denbrock. We started talking. Coach Denbrock said: What are your thoughts about Willingham? Are you going to bad mouth him? Are you going to bad mouth the program? I couldn't believe what I was hearing. I told them that I wouldn't.

"So I did my pro day there at Washington. Scouts got a chance to look at me. I felt like I was blessed to be given the opportunity to run for them. Then a few days later, I heard from my agent that Willingham was bad mouthing me to scouts. The word around the camp fire is that I was uncoachable, bad attitude, stay away from this guy.

"I go to a NFL website and look up my name. It says in little quotations, tall, rangy guy, good size and speed, has authority issues, reportedly cussed out a coach. I asked Coach J.D. [Williams], and he said nobody asked him about that situation, but even if they did he would never say anything about that. It was Willingham. I was like, well that sucks. I kept my mouth shut about you, the least you could do is give a good report to the scouts. I never spoke to Willingham again. I never saw him again."

Unlike three other members of the same UW secondary that went on to the NFL, Hemphill has played the past three seasons in the Arena League. "When I was growing up in Los Angeles I always watched Washington on TV," he says. "When I see the Husky games now I feel that's my team. I still know a few guys on the team and I still talk with them. I just joined the team during a rough spot. They've got a good coach now and they're going to work hard and get back to where they need to be."

Hemphill still harbors NFL dreams while trying to remain positive about his experience as a Husky. "Coach Willingham did touch my life," he said. "Not in a good way, but it made me appreciate things more. I had a scholarship and it made me appreciate having been a Division I player. To go down to Division II and see the travel situation, food situation, scarcity of equipment, I saw that I had been spoiled at Washington. Even though we didn't have the gourmet meals at Central that we had at Washington, we still had that camaraderie and the coaches understood the players. It was a good experience at Central. I would have never known that if I had stayed at Washington the whole time. It showed me the other side. Everybody is not fortunate enough to be at USC or Washington."

Placekicker Michael Braunstein

CHAPTER 13

A Visit with Michael Braunstein

Michael Braunstein was an outspoken placekicker who played for the Huskies from 2003-2006. He earned All Pac-10 academic honorable mention all four seasons. In 2006, he connected on 10 of 12 field goals and was 32 of 32 on extra points, and was recognized as honorable mention All Pac-10. At the end of that season Willingham dismissed him from the team. Braunstein went on to play for Ohio and Frank Solich for his senior season of 2007. He became a Lou Groza Award Semifinalist and was named first team All-Mac Selection. He earned Academic All-Mac honors while completing a Masters Degree. He made 20 of 24 field goals and all 38 PATs attempted. This included a nation-leading streak of 20 consecutive field goals made.

Braunstein's sometimes abrasive personality was best summed up by Husky teammate Johnie Kirton: "Mike is the little short man who is an asshole to everybody. But once you break through that barrier, Mike is one of the funniest dudes and is cool. I never blamed Mike for his bitterness, because one man comes in and says I don't like your approach, you're out of here. That kind of thing is not right to a guy who has put blood, sweat and tears into a program."

Derek Johnson: What was your first reaction when Willingham arrived at Washington?

Michael Braunstein: When he arrived we wondered why is this guy talking in the third person? But more or less we were excited to get a new coach. Everything was screwed up from when Rick [Neuheisel] gave us our scholarships and then disappeared, and then we got stuck with [Keith Gilbertson] for two years. It was nice to have a new regime with the hope that things were moving in the right direction. But that hope went away pretty quick.

Johnson: I heard you were a regular attendee of Willingham's disciplinary Sunday morning workouts, otherwise known as the Breakfast Club.

Braunstein: (*uproarious laughter*) I think me and Chris Hemphill were the presidents of the Breakfast Club. That was one of the biggest gripes I had with Willingham. Missing a lift, getting in trouble in class, not attending class, that's his reasoning for putting you in the Breakfast Club. When is the Breakfast Club? It's at 6:30 AM on Sunday morning. If you're a college kid what are you doing on Saturday night? You're going out. But what does a kid do on Sunday morning after he gets his ass kicked for two hours in workouts while Tyrone swings his golf club and we do a bunch of gay-ass drills? What do you think we go home and do for the rest of the day?

Johnson: Probably went straight to sleep.

Braunstein: Exactly. What do you think every other college player in America is doing on Sunday? Studying. So why are we in punishment? Because we missed class or got in trouble in his eyes. Rather than a Frank Solich, who I played for at Ohio and consider him the best coach I ever had. If you miss class you wake up at 6:30 AM on a school day and come into his office and you study in his office with him. And he gives you a nice little chat on your way out the door. Now, I was never in that because I was there getting my Masters Degree. But that's what other guys told me.

Johnson: So how would you end up in The Breakfast Club?

Braunstein: We had parties we threw at our house. We threw some big parties. We were known as the party house. I was considered the lead on that. I lived with Cody Ellis, Durrell Moss, Taj Bohmar, Juan Garcia. We all lived together. Willingham heard about those parties and I got put into The Breakfast Club two or three times for that. I got in trouble in class once. Got in trouble for not showing for meals.

You had to go to training table. An article came out in the paper once, it was feature on me. It was one of those "cocky kicker" articles. Willingham called me into his office and had the article there with notations. He wanted to know why I said something and I told him it was taken out of context—I told him that in order to cover my ass. But it didn't work, and I was back in The Breakfast Club.

Johnson: I've heard you had clashes with strength and conditioning coach Trent Greener.

Braunstein: I'm a placekicker, why do I need to do a bench press? They wouldn't tailor workouts to me for my position, they wanted me to do the same lift an offensive lineman would lift. It was bullshit. It wasn't like that when Steve Emtman was there with Pete Kaligis as strength coaches.

Johnson: So you got along well with Steve and respected him?

Braunstein: Oh yeah, I loved Steve. Later on I played [in the Arena League] against Steve's team that he owned. I talked to him a lot. I talked to him one night at The Red Door in Fremont about two weeks after Willingham had fired him. We both had a few drinks. That was a fun conversation.

Johnson: Any particulars?

Braunstein: Steve was just pissed off. He was mad that he had given so much blood, sweat and tears to the program and then was told that he was no longer wanted there. Willingham didn't want him around at all. Steve said that Willingham told him he would give him some sort of severance pay. Steve couldn't believe it, because Steve has a ton of money. He and Willingham got into a big fight. Steve was like, "Do you think I was in this for the fucking money? I'm doing this to help the kids. I'm doing this because I'm a Dawg for life."

Johnson: Through my interviews with dozens of former Huskies I still haven't come to understand why people went into the Willingham doghouse.

Braunstein: Body language. The body language they would exhibit.

Willingham took mental notes not so much about how we were playing but how we were acting. He wanted people showing proper deference to him. If you weren't a soldier then you weren't one of his favorites. You had to be a soldier in order to get playing time.

Johnson: When you and I talked a couple years ago, you referred to Jake Locker as one of Willingham's soldiers.

Braunstein: (*laughs*) It's not that Jake was a soldier. Jake is a great kid. He's an all-star in everything he does. Willingham wanted a team of Jake Lockers. I don't mean that as an athlete, because everyone wants a team of Jake Lockers as athletes. But I mean his demeanor. How Jake went about his business. He didn't ever speak his mind. He did what he was told and did it well.

Johnson: Former Husky and current UW employee Greg Lewis said he didn't know anything was wrong between players and Willingham until he had a long conversation with Scott White at the end of 2006.

Braunstein: No, if guys went and talked to a Greg Lewis or an academic counselor and it got back to Willingham, you would get in trouble and wouldn't play. It was over for you. Willingham became the program. It was his face on the media guide. It was his face on the side of the stadium with that giant fucking poster. It was his face on the ticket campaign. His face was everywhere.

Johnson: I wonder if that was what UW thought they were getting when they brought in Willingham to clean up the program?

Braunstein: What was there to clean up? I don't know what was going on that needed cleaning. Shit, we didn't have guys going to jail or anything like that. What Willingham did was make everybody scared to even walk. He made everybody scared of making a mistake.

Willingham would be a great coach at Air Force, Navy, Army or Yale. I think he would flourish as a coach at those places. Those guys are soldiers and will do everything they are told. He had no idea how to communicate with the kind of student-athletes at Washington. Everything was his way or the highway. We loathed everything about playing for him. Oh God, we've got to go to practice again? There was no fun, no excitement.

Johnson: You once told me that some players didn't even want to go to a bowl game late in the 2006 season.

Braunstein: Exactly! Hell yeah. That was our chatter as we're sitting there in full gear about to go out there to practice, and talking about how we had a chance to go to a bowl game. Some guys were going "Do we really want to go to a bowl game? That would mean three more weeks of practice for this guy. We don't need a bowl game that badly, who cares?"

Johnson: Toward the end of the 2006 season Willingham dropped you from the team in the Suddenly Senior situation. You played your senior season for Ohio.

Braunstein: I had a great senior season and was a Lou Grozza Semi-Finalist, which goes to the best kicker in America. I'm a Husky and a Dawg for life and all that, but the most fun I ever had playing football was that senior year playing for Frank Solich at Ohio. Our stadium held 19,000 fans so it wasn't anything like Husky Stadium of course. But it was a smaller town and we were treated well. It was great to enjoy playing football again.

CHAPTER 14

Birth of the Mora Revolution

"A revolution is an idea which has found its bayonets."

—Napoleon Bonaparte

A victory over Washington State may have served as a salve to the six game losing streak, but the 2006 season disappointed from all vantage points. The 5-7 record marked the first time Washington had suffered three consecutive losing seasons since the mid-1950s. Willingham also engendered a measure of anger in the fan base for his handling of the Suddenly Senior situation. In spite of this, Husky Nation largely remained in his corner.

Tyrone's stoic stance gave no hint of concern. Athletic director Todd Turner, when questioned by media at season's end, remained resolute. "I'm sticking with a guy who's been there before. A guy who's tough, who's smart, who's principled. He isn't learning on the job. He's done this before, so I have complete confidence in him. I have no concern whatsoever in his ability to take us where we need to go. I'm just not sure about the timing of it... I won't second-guess him. He knows what he's doing."

In reality, both Willingham and Turner weren't so self-confident. Both displayed irritation during the Suddenly Senior scrutiny. Now with the season over, they yearned for the dust to settle. The last thing they needed was another controversy.

Across the country, former Husky linebacker Jim L. Mora was coaching the NFL's Atlanta Falcons. Coming off their 17-6 win over Tampa Bay on December 10th, the Falcons were 7-6 and clawing for a wild card position in the playoffs. As a passionate alumnus of the

University of Washington, Mora's roots ran deep in Husky soil. His father had been a defensive coordinator for Washington under Don James in the 1970s. During Mora's childhood, his babysitter was Don James' daughter. When Mora fulfilled his dream in the early 1980s to play for the Huskies, he never rose above the status of backup linebacker. However, he had the opportunity to play in two Rose Bowls and was a popular member of the Lambda Chi Alpha fraternity. In fact, his popularity earned him the nickname "Rump Daddy" from the UW women's track team.

After graduating from Washington, Mora served as a graduate assistant for Don James before landing an assistant job with the NFL's San Diego Chargers in 1985. Over time, he moved up in the world. First he headed to New Orleans as a secondary coach, then on to the San Francisco 49ers, where he eventually became defensive coordinator in 2003. He was largely viewed as a charismatic guy with a bright defensive mind.

Former Husky Hugh Millen certainly praised Mora to the hilt. In a 2004 interview with Greg Bishop of *The Seattle Times*, Millen spoke in grandiose terms about his former college teammate and roommate. "He is a coach without a flaw," he said. "He's going to be one of the greats in this industry. Twenty years from now, people are going to talk about him as one of the great, all-time coaches. Ever. Twenty-five years from now they'll be handing him a yellow blazer."

But yellow blazers were the last thing on Mora's mind in December 2006. His team closed out the season with a three game losing streak to finish the season with a 7-9 record. For a team that had harbored playoff aspirations, it was a crushing disappointment.

As bad as that was, it represented only half of Mora's troubles. The other half stemmed from a December interview with Dave "Softy" Mahler and Hugh Millen in a segment for sports radio KJR in Seattle. It was given while the Falcons were 7-6 and still playoff eligible. Things got interesting at the halfway point, when Mahler jokingly told Mora if there was ever an opening at Washington, he wanted him to come back to coach the Huskies.

"Well, I really have a lot of respect for Ty, and I know he'll do a great job," Mora said. "But if he ever decides to move on, and get in the NFL or you know, go back to Notre Dame or whatever, if that job's open you'll find me at the friggin' head of the line with my resume in my hand ready to take that job."

"If you're available," Mahler said.

"It doesn't even matter if I'm available."

Hugh Millen then chimed in. "So if you just won the Super Bowl, and it's available, you're there?"

"I'd be there," said Mora.

"You're there, okay," said Millen.

"Dewey, I promise you that. Now, I want to see Ty succeed, and I want to see that program succeed. But if he decides at some point that he's ready to move on and they want me, I will be there. I don't care if we're in the middle of a playoff run, I'm packing my stuff and coming back to Seattle."

A stunned Mahler said, "So, are you saying..."

"You know, it's funny. And I mean that, and I'm dead serious, the further I get away from it the more I'm drawn to it. You know, that's the job I want, so..."

"You would leave the Falcons for that job?"

"Absolutely."

"Wow," exclaimed Mahler.

"As I'm sitting here, I'm looking at a Huskies helmet."

The media maelstrom was instantaneous. Atlanta Fans howled in angry protest. Falcon owner Arthur Blank summoned Mora to his office for a stern talk, before sending the coach out alone to face the media. Mora fully knew he'd let the horses out of barn. "I thought [it sounded like] I was kidding but in listening to the replay it certainly didn't sound like that," Mora said to reporters. "So I apologize. I certainly didn't want to offend anyone in Atlanta here with the Falcons, Ty Willingham, or people in Seattle. It was just very poor judgment on my part and for that I apologize."

Fans and media weren't biting. They climbed all over him. The national press too. Up in Seattle, media prodded Willingham for a reaction. "As I heard one of the commentators say, that was a great case of opening mouth and inserting foot," Willingham said.

For Husky fans who felt the Willingham act was wearing thin, the idea of the fireball Mora taking over was intoxicating. "It was my best moment in Husky Football since the 2001 Rose Bowl," said Race Bannon, co-host of the *Husky Half Brain Podcast.* "You could feel Mora's love for Husky football coming through the radio." Message boards and radio airwaves crackled to life, brimming with speculation and possibility. The first debates began to rage between Willingham supporters and Willingham doubters. In time, this chasm would only grow.

Unfortunately for Mora, the chasm between him and the Atlanta organization had grown irreconcilably wide. On January 2, 2007, the Falcons fired him. "This was an extremely difficult decision for us," Blank said in a prepared statement. "We had the highest hopes and aspirations for a long run with Jim as our coach, but we feel this decision is in the best long-term interests of our franchise. I have great respect for Jim's passion for the game, and we wish Jim and his family all of the best."

Three weeks later, the headline of *The Seattle Times* sports section read: "Seahawks Hire Ex-Husky Mora as Assistant Head Coach."

W

Freshman quarterback Jake Locker

CHAPTER 15

Enter the Savior

"All is not broken at Washington. It's not in as bad shape as people in the country make it out to be. It's really in pretty good shape."

—Todd Turner, UW athletic director, 2004

IN late August 2007, amid the bright sunshine at Husky Stadium, the line of fans greeting Jake Locker's table at UW's Picture Day stretched from one sideline to the other. The redshirt freshman-to-be seemed a bit embarrassed by the whole thing. "It was definitely kind of surprising," Locker said to a reporter. "I didn't really understand it. I haven't played any games yet."

The Locker name was synonymous with small-town Ferndale, where he quarterbacked the Ferndale Golden Eagles to the 2005 Class 3A state title. In that season, Locker possessed a 27:3 touchdown-to-interception ratio and scored 24 rushing touchdowns. *Parade Magazine* recognized him as a first-team All-American. At the 2007 Pac-10 media day, Arizona State coach Dennis Erickson gushed over Locker, calling him the best high-school quarterback he had ever seen. "You get a guy of his talent, that turns programs around pretty damn fast," Erickson said. "The biggest thing [Washington] ever did was get him. He can turn that program around."

With Locker's emergence on the scene, optimism ran high among the fan base. The odd and disappointing thing was Turner's tendency to lower expectations. He said the Huskies could win fewer games than the year before but still have improved. "I like what I see on the field," he said to the media. "And I really like what I see off the field in terms of creating the kind of culture here that will sustain itself for a long period of time. If you were to really pin coach Willingham down, he would probably tell you that he was surprised there was as much work to be done to bring everybody back together. Our players lacked focus and commitment and unity—all the things coach Willingham is bringing to the program. It's taken a while, and we're still a work in progress. We're nowhere near where we need to be, though we are closer… What people need to understand is that this is a very, very difficult rebuilding job, maybe as difficult as any in the country for a number of reasons."

Willingham, too, nourished ways to deflate enthusiasm. The 2007 season opener, against Syracuse in the Carrier Dome, was like a dream. As the nation watched on ESPN, Locker shone in breath-taking fashion. He ran with moves that even great running backs don't possess. His passing was accurate, going 14 for 19. Running back Louis Rankin ran wild in space, and Washington crushed Syracuse 42-12. In the bedlam of the locker room, joyful players broke out the infamous "Say Who?" chant. It had been invented by UW linebacker Antowaine Richardson in the 1970s, and was used to psyche the team up, especially after victories. In the Willingham era victories had been a sparse commodity, so it seemed a great time to roll it out.

Say Who? (Say Who!)
Say What? (Say What!)
Say who say Dawgs ain't bad motherfuckers!
Say Who? (Say Who!)
Say What? (Say What!)
Say who say Dawgs ain't bad motherfuckers!

Tyrone Willingham held up his hand and shouted for everyone to stop. The locker room fell silent. Willingham reminded them cursing wasn't permitted. They needed to amend the chant in order to continue it. "Replace that curse word with mamma jamma," Willingham said.

"Willingham was all about no cussing," said defensive end Caesar Rayford. "The Say Who, Say What chant, that's who we were and what we were about. We wanted to be motherfuckers. We didn't want to be mamma jammas. Who wants to be a mamma jamma? We tried chanting it, but mamma jamma? It didn't even sound right. We ended up giving Willingham blank stares."

The following Saturday saw Boise State arrive at Husky Stadium with a 14-game winning streak—the nation's longest. Ranked #20 in the country, the Broncos had been the nation's darlings the previous January, when they stunned heavily-favored Oklahoma in the Fiesta Bowl. That had been one of the most exciting bowl games ever played, and what stood out was the assortment of play-calling chicanery pulled off by Boise State, including an unforgettable Statue-of-Liberty play to win the game.

70,045 spectators, including a healthy contingent of Bronco fans, nearly filled Husky Stadium. Boise State racked up over 450 yards of offense, but repeatedly turned the ball over inside of Washington's red zone. Just as influential to the outcome was Boise State's inability to stop Jake Locker. The Husky QB single-handedly kept the chains moving and sustained drives with his physical and elusive running style. Washington won 24-10, to move their record to 2-0. It served as the Huskies' first win over a ranked team since 2003 and marked the most significant win in the Willingham era.

"We have our swagger back," boasted receiver Marcel Reece who had been on the receiving end of a 58-yard touchdown reception. "The Huskies are back. We are walking with our heads up and walking with a lot of confidence."

Copious amounts of confidence would be needed the following week, as Coach Jim Tressell's tenth-ranked Ohio State Buckeyes came to Husky Stadium in a nationally televised contest. Washington's fan base screamed their lungs out, giving all the help they could to the Husky defense, and Washington led 7-3 at halftime. But come the second half, everything unraveled. The Buckeyes ran the football at will and controlled the clock, blasting the Huskies 33-14.

Fans and local the media immediately took solace that the Huskies hung close until halftime against a powerhouse opponent. That lasted until Monday morning, when an article appeared on Dawgman.com. Former Husky Tim Meamber had been a first team All Pac-10 linebacker for the 1984 Huskies that won the Orange Bowl over Oklahoma.

The article, entitled "Tim Meamber Analyzes the Defense," gave him a platform to air his views.

"I watched the game from the end zone," Meamber was quoted as saying, "so I can read the guards from a linebacker's perspective. I'm telling you, our inside linebackers don't read both guards. If you don't read both guards, the offense is going to start trapping. And if the offense starts trapping while your inside linebackers aren't reading both guards, your backers are going to get creamed by the offensive tackles coming down—and that creates large holes in the defense.

"Ohio State came out running power runs right at us," he said. "Then in the second quarter they started doing a little trapping. Once they started trapping, they realized that their tackles were getting down on our middle backers. We never adjusted. At that point, it became very evident to me that Ohio State was going to run traps all day long—and that's what they did. I think our linebackers must be keying on the backfield. And that runs contrary to everything that [former UW defensive coordinator] Jim Lambright taught us and what I know to be right about playing linebacker… The thing to remember is that an offensive line only has about eight blocking schemes, and the entire line has to block in unison on each of them. As a defender, once you develop a knowledge of that, then you can make plays.

"On defense, we are missing leadership. When the team got tired against Ohio State, everyone was flat. I am waiting for someone to emerge as a leader on that defense. When you're tired, that's when you've got to play with emotion. The things that I don't see are the emotion, enthusiasm, intensity and leadership on the Husky defense. Against Ohio State, our defense got tired and was just standing there waiting for the offense to break the huddle. Right there, somebody's got to take charge, and fire our guys up! They need to say, 'Let's get the hell off the field–NOW!' Heading into the fourth quarter, we looked mentally, physically and emotionally defeated. Everyone in the stadium knew it was over. Why? Because our team looked defeated and our defense looked defeated.

"You also don't see enough emotion from them when they come out of the tunnel. That tunnel is hallowed, sacred ground. I don't care if what I'm saying is politically incorrect. They did away with the 'Say

Who' chant several years ago because it was considered too profane. Well, I don't care if the players have to run 10 fucking 100s, the 'Say Who' chant has got to come back! It starts with that chant, it's Husky tradition. I don't care if the University President tells them to stop it, they've got to get that intensity back! I don't care what the sanctions are. That chant and that mentality gets you jacked up, it intimidates the opponent. The whole tunnel echoes with that chant. Who cares what the non-football people say. Get it done!"

Reverberations from the article hit local sports radio programming and Husky football message boards. Willingham didn't care for the public dressing down. The topic was raised that evening, on the *Tyrone Willingham Show*, a radio program that ran weekly during the season at a Seattle-area restaurant called Anthony's Home Port. The head coach bristled at the sudden scrutiny.

A week later, following a loss to USC, Willingham himself fanned the flames of discord. While addressing the media, he stated he needed "more bullets" in order to compete. When asked to extrapolate, Willingham referred to the Trojans' roster. "How many of our players could start for USC?" A moment later he answered his own question, off the record. "Jake Locker is the only player on our team that could start for USC."

But the comment about needing "more bullets" got into the newspapers, and many Washington players raged upon reading it. One of them, Johnie Kirton, sought Willingham out in his office. "He said he felt bad about what he had said, and I think it was because his mind wasn't there," Kirton said. "Any man or woman can say something stupid and you can forgive them if their mindset isn't right. I know it wasn't really what he wanted to say, but I wanted to hear it from him. I felt like he was showing humility. I was one of the few guys who butted heads with him constantly. And for him to show humility to me, that told me that it was probably genuine. But his comments were divisive, and that created a bigger division between him and the players."

Perhaps it was that divisiveness that explained how Washington, despite having two weeks to prepare for a game in Tempe against Arizona State, could get blown out 44-20. ASU's starting tailback Ryan Torain was sidelined due to injury, but that didn't stop the second and third string running backs from each topping 100 yards against the Husky defense. Keegan Herring and Dimitri Nance ran wild in the warm desert night. In the second half alone, ASU rushed for 227 yards and outscored Washington 31-3. As the game concluded, the scene was once again reminiscent of Groundhog Day. Despondent Huskies trudged off the field with heads down and vacant stares. Receding quickly from memory was the 2-0 start to the season. The dread of another avalanche of losses took its place.

"That's a tough locker room," said Tyrone Willingham after the game. "Because that should be a very disappointed locker room that I just walked out of, which it was. Gosh, they don't have an explanation, I don't have an explanation for our third quarter, why we are right there, and why we do some things, or a series of things, that let it get away."

With Washington's fortunes falling by the wayside, the Huskies prepared to take on the rival Oregon Ducks on October 20th in Husky Stadium. During the pre-game radio show on KJR, athletic director Todd Turner engaged in his usual pre-game interview with Dave "Softy" Mahler, Dick Baird and Hugh Millen. The Ducks entered the game as the nation's seventh-ranked team. The hosts expressed concern that Oregon had destroyed Washington for three years in a row, but Turner said he wasn't worried. He knew that the Huskies would win. When asked why, Turner replied: "Because today I'm wearing my lucky purple shoes."

As the teams lined up and the opening kickoff sailed through the air, not even Turner's lucky purple shoes could fend off Oregon's offensive juggernaut. The Ducks racked up 665 total yards, including a school-record 461 yards on the ground. Jonathan Stewart, the local prep running back who spurned Washington to go to Oregon, tallied 251 yards and 2 touchdowns. On one scoring play, Duck quarterback Dennis Dixon could be seen laughing as he rolled out and tossed an easy lob to a wide open receiver in the end zone.

The game was men against boys. Washington's lone bright spot was the performance of Jake Locker, largely on broken plays. Though only 12 of 31 through the air, Locker threw for 257 yards, ran for 78 yards, and scored 4 touchdowns. He single-handedly tied the game at 31-31 with 1:12 left in the third quarter.

But the Ducks crushed the Huskies 24-3 in the final quarter, cruising to an easy 55-34 win. Oregon's 55 points were the second most scored by an opponent in Husky Stadium history—second only to California's 56 points scored in Willingham's first year at Washington. The loss left Washington with the nation's 118th ranked defense against the run.

For the first time, fans began making their anger truly felt. Todd Turner took to his *Top Dawg Blog*, scolding the fans for being too focused on winning, and calling on them to be true fans. That week in *The Seattle Times*, Turner again stressed to columnist Steve Kelley the need to support Willingham. "He is the right person at the right time… this is a long, arduous process, and I'm very confident in Coach Willingham's ability to turn it around. Tyrone doesn't need my vote of confidence. This is as tough a situation as I've ever seen in my career. Tyrone is just at the beginning of his voyage. This is a hard and competitive league, and you don't just wish to get better. It takes time. It takes patience. It starts with what you believe in. This is a culture that wants immediate gratification. Unfortunately some things take diligence, and time, and hard work."

Kelley concluded the article by concurring, "…the mistakes are repeating themselves. Missed tackles. Dropped passes. Busted running plays. Blown pass coverages. Still, Turner is right. No coach in the country inherited as massive a rebuilding job as Willingham."

The following Saturday, hapless Arizona ventured into Husky Stadium. Rumors of an imminent firing swirled about their coach Mike Stoops. This game served as a clash between Pac-10 doormats. Prior to the game, as the Huskies sat in their team room, the door swung open from the tunnel. Several Wildcat players crammed in the doorway, taunting the Huskies with yelps and feeble barking. Husky players got angry, but Willingham ordered them not to retaliate. "Let's do our talking on the field," he told his team.

At one point in the game, it seemed history might be in the making. Jake Locker was running circles around the Arizona defense, largely on broken plays. UW radio announcer Bob Rondeau likened it to Marques Tuiasosopo's performance in 1999, when he became the only player in college football division I history to pass for 300 yards and rush for 200 yards in the same game. He had done it against Tyrone Willingham's Stanford team in 1999.

With 11:32 remaining in the game, Washington led 41-26 and victory seemed imminent. But fans could only watch in horror as the final minutes unfurled. Arizona quarterback Willie Tuitama threw for three of his five touchdown passes as the Wildcats outscored the Huskies 22-6 in the fourth quarter, to win 48-41. Tuitama capped the day with 510 yards passing, the most ever against Washington, and tied for seventh-most in Pac-10 history. For the first time in recent memory, fans unleashed a torrent of boos as the Huskies and Willingham left the field and entered the tunnel. As UW fullback Paul Homer reached his locker, he sat down and sobbed.

Washington's record fell to 2-6 overall and 0-5 in the Pac-10 Conference. Tyrone Willingham's mark as Husky coach sat at 9-22. "I think it goes without saying that this one is very, very difficult," he said afterward. "I am extremely disappointed."

Thousands of fans lost all faith in Willingham that day. As those in attendance filed out of the stadium, a funeral-like pall hung in the air. For the third straight season, Washington was in the throes of a six-game losing streak.

As long-time Husky fan Ron Johnson drove home from the game, his hands gripped the steering wheel with frustration not seen since the 1995 Washington-Oregon game. He had been a season ticket holder since 1957, and stuck with the Dawgs through thick and thin. He had seen the Huskies play in ten Rose Bowls, and remained steadfast with them through bad times too. But now he couldn't bear the depths to which the program had sunk. As he reached the I-90 Floating Bridge, he entertained a startling thought: *Why not give up the tickets and stop subjecting myself to this endless torture?* But by the time he reached the other side of Lake Washington, the thought dissipated. "I couldn't give up the tickets," he said. "I love the Huskies and Jake Locker too much."

Tailback Kenny James (8), quarterback Carl Bonnell (11) and center Juan Garcia (58)

Linebackers Mason Foster and E.J. Savannah

WASHINGTON HUSKIES

UNIVERSITY OF WASHINGTON FOOTBALL
Graves Annex, Box 354080, Seattle Washington 98195-4080
206 221-2896 fax 206 616-1926 email football@u.washington.edu

October 19, 2006

To Whom It May Concern:

This letter is to recommend Michael Braunstein. Michael has been a member of the football team since fall of 2003. He has been under my tutelage for the past two football seasons.

He has shown himself to be a bright and intelligent young man. He has found ways to incorporate himself into the team despite his position which limits his overall interaction. Michael has also shown the ability to be creative within his position. Upon having a conversation with all of our kickers regarding creating a variety of kicks, Michael took it upon himself to develop some unique kicks that have been blended into our game plan and in one case instrumental to us winning the game.

He has consistently been one of our better students and possesses a quick mind with a good sense of humor. As you review your pool of applicants, I hope you'll find room for a bright, energetic young man who gives of himself tirelessly and doesn't know the meaning of the word quit. I know you will be pleased with what Michael will bring to your program.

Sincerely,

Tyrone Willingham
Head Football Coach

TW: eaz

www.gohuskies.com 2001 ROSEBOWL CHAMPIONS

Tyrone Willingham's letter of recommendation for Michael Braunstein, less than two weeks before taking away his senior season

Hawaii quarterback Colt Brennan torched a hapless
Husky defense for 442 yards in a December 2007 game

Defensive end Daniel Teo-Nesheim

Defensive back Roy Lewis was so disgusted with Tyrone Willingham he almost quit football to become a firefighter

Linebacker Dan Howell

Husky fan Jason Pingree placed signs outside of Husky Stadium and the Graves Building as the Mora Revolution was underway

Athletic Director Todd Turner (foreground) and the sparse crowd at the 2006 Stanford game acknowledge former Husky Steve Emtman's entry into the College Football Hall of Fame

Jordan Reffert comforts Tahj Bomar in the final seconds of a humiliating loss to Stanford in 2006

The Husky Marching Band

Linebacker Mason Foster leads the Way

Hugh Millen (right) with his former college coach Don James

CHAPTER 16

The Miseducation of Jake Locker

Hugh Millen played quarterback for the Huskies in the 1980s and is best known for leading Washington to a victory over Oklahoma in the 1985 Orange Bowl. After being drafted by the Los Angeles Rams, Millen played for eleven years and picked up a Super Bowl ring as a member of the 1993 Dallas Cowboys. Millen now works as a football analyst for KJR-AM radio and KCPQ television in Seattle, Washington.

When Jake Locker arrived at Washington in 2006 as a redshirt freshman quarterback, Millen marveled at the young man's ability to run and throw as well as his strength and startling humbleness. For the next three seasons, Millen was in the unique position of being one of the few able to attend UW practices while having a higher level of comprehension of what was taking place.

Derek Johnson: What's your take on Jake Locker's time spent playing for Tyrone Willingham?

Hugh Millen: In my opinion, Jake Locker is the greatest athlete to ever come out of the state of Washington. If your boat is taking on water, you can either bail it out with a coffee can, or with a modern day hydraulic pump. Locker is like the hydraulic pump. As I saw it, Tyrone didn't know how to effectively use that pump. That's what Jake Locker was to me. The most capable tool or means to bail the Huskies out of the hole, and we had a guy who had very little idea how to use it.

I wasn't a great player, I wasn't even a good player in the NFL. But

I was around great coaches and quarterbacks and receivers. I think I counted twenty-four Pro Bowl players from those three positions. Let alone like playing for coaches like Don James, Mike Shanahan, Jimmy Johnson, Ernie Zampese and Norv Turner. All you have to do is pay attention around that kind of greatness to learn a little.

Johnson: So you weren't an All-Pro, but you were the MVP of the '91 Patriots and after that season signed the largest contract in franchise history. And eleven years in the NFL is a lot of time to soak up valuable information.

Millen: But I was primarily a backup. I will be the first one to tell you that if it's just about my playing career, I don't have much qualification. However, if there's such a thing as an *observing* career, that would probably be my perspective in this interview. My years *observing* in the NFL enabled me to see and learn just enough to make me angry about the meager coaching of Locker during the Willingham years. I watched how the passing game was being coached under Willingham and it was night and day with how Steve Sarkisian is coaching Jake now. Sarkisian is employing the effective coaching techniques with Jake and it's just what Jake needs. I just hope it's not too late. I would love to see how Jake's career would have been if Sarkisian had coached him for five years.

Johnson: Please give your perception of Locker's tutelage under Willingham.

Millen: Offensive coordinator Tim Lappano and Luke Huard were the ones in Jake's ear. So you've got in one a former running back and in the other a graduate assistant who played for two years at North Carolina. In my experience, what you need is somebody in there who's got the hammer to say to the receivers: "LOOK, you have to run it here, at this depth, at this angle, this is expected of you—the QB is expecting this of you. Get the job done, no excuses." You've got to have a guy who can bring that hammer in the offensive meeting room and on the field. With Lappano and Huard they didn't appear to have that.

If you've played the quarterback position, you can see it and feel it, whether a guy is wrong with his steps or his balance. It's not something you just see, you feel it. It's like a golf coach. To be Tiger Woods's swing coach, you don't have to have won six majors on the PGA tour. But you had better be a scratch golfer or close to it. So when those coaches see a pro's swing, they're not just looking at the swing, they're *feeling* it. They say "Oh, you've got the club too far inside," or whatever. They translate their eye to their muscle memory. They feel how that club would be lost inside and how hard it would be to get it around.

So it goes with the passing game. When Steve Sarkisian and [current offensive coordinator] Doug Nussmeier are working with the passing game, they know whether the feet are getting too wide, what the timing should be, when the ball should be released. A guy who has played the position feels it. And when they stand just a few yards behind Jake during team drills in practice, they can spot these things. They see downfield and they know where the quarterback's eyes should be and when. They feel mistakes with the quarterback's mechanics.

Lappano had been a very talented under-sized running back/scat back during his playing days. Sure, he could study the passing game, but at about 5'9"standing behind the pass pocket during practice, I believe it had to have been nearly impossible for him to feel the precise execution necessary in the passing game and be able to communicate that to a top-flight quarterback. I question whether Lappano had much of a sense of what the quarterback could even see during those drills and how that might affect the qb's progressions. Moreover, Luke Huard didn't have the hammer because he was only a GA. Jake Locker is a world class athlete with the potential to be an elite quarterback. Under Willingham, I don't believe they had anybody there who could take him to the next level.

Johnson: Are there specific examples you can give?

Millen: I remember one time in practice when Jake goes back, takes a five-step drop, takes a hitch, throws a seam route down the middle. The ball is caught 28 yards down the field from the line of scrimmage. It's a beautiful throw, but it can't win. It's too late. The ball has to be caught no more than 22 yards down the field. But here it is caught 6 yards too deep. In a game the safety will blow up the play. Or the play-side corner could fall off of his zone and make a play. It cannot time up.

It was a beautiful pass, a laser, a tight spiral, hits the guy in stride. It looks like that with the run after catch it will be a 40-50 yard gain. But it's wrong. It's unacceptable by anyone with high standards. Then Jake walks back to the huddle. He gets a high five from Luke Huard, he gets a high five from Lappano. And Lappano is then looking at his play-sheet to call the next play for the next quarterback. Jake gets back in line. He gets a couple of more high fives from his teammates and stands there watching the next play. Nobody talks to him. Lappano is too busy coordinating the drill. Locker, on the surface of it, appeared to have had a heck of a pass. Even to his teammate's eyes, it was a heck of a pass. Nobody is telling him it can't work. But his feet were too late, he can't take an extra hitch. Even at 24 yards, a coach has to be on you: "Hey that's two yards too deep!" That's the difference between a completion and a hospital ball, where the tight end is looking for his mouthpiece. Let me emphasize this point: Coaches often prefer to coach precise detail in the film room to maintain an effective pace of practice. But those coaches don't respond to unacceptable execution on the field with a smile and a high-five.

Johnson: Do you have other examples?

Millen: Numerous. Another time involved a corner route. It's going west-to-east in Husky Stadium [toward Lake Washington]. Ball is on the 25-yard line. It's a smash route, with an inside corner route to the slot receiver with Jake throwing to his left. This is in skeleton (no offensive and defensive linemen, just the quarterback and five eligible receivers versus linebackers and defensive backs). Jake drops back and takes two hitches. He completes the pass and beats the defense for about a 20-yard gain. Again, high fives from Lappano, high fives from Huard, and a couple more from his teammates. Somebody needed to say: "Jake, that was a hell of a throw, but it was against Quarters coverage, with the weak linebacker sunk inside. He didn't get his depth. It was wide open out there. Against that defense you could have taken three hitches and still have completed it. We're not trying to just beat a defense against a semi-blown coverage in practice. We're trying to have timing that gives us the maximum probability of beating all coverages in actual games. Jake, you were much too late with that pass. We need to force the timing. Take seven steps, take one quick hitch and get rid of it. Force yourself to have the timing to have the best chance to beat the maximum number of defenses. Taking two hitches on a corner route and eyeballing the receiver won't cut it."

In Jake's defense, on the various pass-routes, ten different receivers would run ten different angles and route depths. He didn't know exactly where they were going. He didn't know at what spot they would be. So he would tend to eyeball his receivers, which introduced a whole new problem because doing so will usually draw the defense to the intended receiver.

Johnson: That explains a lot. You've mentioned timing issues. Were there other concerns?

Millen: There was a game against Oregon State. The Huskies were repeatedly max-protecting although the Beavers were only rushing four guys. So there were only two or three Husky receivers in the pattern trying to separate from seven zone defenders. Down after down there were no outlets in the pattern. To the fans the quarterback appears hesitant and out of rhythm but there's no receiver open. The protection scheme doesn't match the rush scheme. On another occasion I recall being on the sideline during pre-game warm-ups at UCLA. The Husky receivers were running slant routes right in front of me. There wasn't one guy who ran the same depth or angle as the others. I watched about eight guys running eight different slant routes. It was just a slant, nothing special. Off the top of my head these are a few of many anecdotes.

Johnson: I remember a conversation you and I had in 2006 where you described cone drills in practice for the Husky wide receivers.

Millen: Those cone drills, as implemented during that time, emphasize chopping your feet and having high shoulders, which is exactly the opposite technique you would want to ingrain [for receivers]. I have always been taught that coming out of a break, if you're going to run an acute angle, you run down the field from the line of scrimmage, and then break at an acute angle either toward the sideline or toward the quarterback. The best technique for separation [from the defensive back] is to run full-stride right up to the last possible yard area – thus presenting the threat of the deep route, then quickly drop your hips, get your chin over your toes, and then explode back on your angle. But the key is that those last steps are preceded by full strides, because that's what is going to push the corner and get separation.

But every day for five days a week they would come out and practice these cone drills. They would have 6-8 choppy steps preceding the break, and their shoulders would rise – which tells the defender the receiver is NOT going deep so the defender then drives on the shorter route. Not only was it wrong in my opinion, it was the opposite of right. Five days a week counter-productive techniques were being ingrained into their muscle memory.

Johnson: I can hear the pain and angst in your voice.

Millen: I'm a Seattle native. I have been a fan of the Mariners since their inception. Same with the Seahawks. I slept on the street to get tickets for the Sonics when they played the Bullets for the 1979 NBA Championship. But if you take all the local teams combined they don't equal how I feel about the Huskies. It's something beyond a sports team. When they suffer I suffer, like so many of us Husky fans do. When they suffer as they have suffered, to me it feels like a death in the family. Somebody can say I've got my priorities misplaced. And I would agree. I'm not equating the Huskies to losing to losing a son or losing my wife. But it's like an extended member of the family and losing him. Perhaps like a cousin. That's what the Willingham years represented to me.

Johnson: You originally were reluctant to participate in this book—I chipped away at you for about six weeks. Why did you decide to offer your commentary on the record?

Millen: Willingham is in the Husky rear-view mirror, so the purpose isn't to shovel more dirt on that pile. For me there are two aspects of this story that remain relevant. One, the 2008 season was so destructive that it's difficult to even process how that could happen. Certainly many factors can be cited but if it's true that exceedingly poor coaching was the substantial reason then that fact actually bodes well for the Huskies moving forward. The Husky football community can view that period as marred but now remedied. Secondly, I hope that [current head coach] Steve Sarkisian can be the Huskies' Bowden or Paterno. From everything that I have seen thus far, I have the opinion that Sarkisian is doing it the right way. But eventually–hopefully decades from now–Washington will have to replace him and I hope we've learned a lesson from having hired Willingham.

Johnson: What lesson?

Millen: Before hiring a coach who had just been fired–particularly from a prominent university–consider thoroughly why he was fired.

Washington State Cougars celebrate their 2007 Apple Cup
win after the Husky defense collapses

CHAPTER 17

Regional Civil War

"It's almost as if the football gods have said: Look, we have heard your pleas, we have seen your pain and we know you're suffering... Here is Jim Mora."

—Race Bannon, Husky Half Brain
Podcast, November 2007

ON the Monday following the complete meltdown loss to Arizona, Washington president Mark Emmert returned to his office and logged onto his computer. A deluge of emails from concerned fans greeted him. Sensing the need to quell the rising storm, he wrote a two-paragraph response that was forwarded to everyone who emailed him.

As a native of Washington and a UW alumnus, I know very well the competitive traditions of our university. Like many of you, I grew up with Husky Football. I share your frustration and disappointment with the team's current position. The same is true of everyone involved with the program.

I also know that the young men on our team are giving the UW everything they have. They are working hard and hanging together during this challenging time. As they do so, I intend to give them my full support and encouragement each and every game. They deserve no less. They are our Huskies, and they should be treated as such. There are five games to be played this season, and our team needs our support.

As the thirtieth president of the University of Washington,

Emmert developed a reputation as one of the most highly-regarded and influential presidents in America. For that fiscal year ending June 30, 2007, Washington received more than $1 billion in grants and contract research funding—the most it had ever received in one year. It furthered Washington's legacy as one of the top public universities in federal research funding for the past forty years.

Although fund raising and public relations were in Emmert's wheelhouse, he also proclaimed a great love of football. Back in 1999, while he was chancellor at Louisiana State University, Emmert fired Curley Hallman as head football coach and lured Nick Saban away from Michigan State. The move paid huge dividends, as LSU won the National Championship in 2003.

Arriving at Washington in 2004, Emmert drew attention to his passion for football when he stated in an interview that he understood football served as the "front porch of the university." Now, following the humiliating loss to Arizona, Emmert had placed himself in the forefront of the public football discourse.

"I understand the passion of football fans," Emmert explained later. "I will never forget being on the field and someone yelled something unkind. My wife remarked to me about it. I told her, 'Gosh honey if I was in the stands I would be yelling it too.' I understood their frustration. I'm a Husky, I was frustrated. Tyrone was frustrated. Everyone knew this was going badly. Everyone felt bad about it."

The month of November proved to be an elixir for the spirits of Willingham supporters. First, there was the 27-9 win over Stanford in Palo Alto, which snapped UW's six-game losing streak. Louis Rankin ran wild, gaining 255 yards rushing—the fourth best in school history. Both players and coaches displayed raw relief and joy. Steve Kelley wrote in *The Seattle Times*: "Willingham needed this. Washington needed this, because, like it or not, the specter of Jim Mora the younger is looming larger and larger over this Washington football program."

The following Saturday, on November 11th, an ambulance removed Jake Locker from Reser Stadium in Corvallis in a game against Oregon State. Locker suffered a neck injury halfway through the second quarter, following a vicious but legal hit from Beaver safety Al Afalava. Subsequent scuffles broke out and three players were ejected, including Washington's Ryan Tolar. Reporters noted it was the most fired up they'd ever seen a Willingham team at Washington. Locker miraculously returned to the sideline in the second half, sporting a neck brace. His presence inspired his teammates, but it wasn't enough as the Beavers won 29-23.

On November 18th, a torrential downpour greeted Washington and the California Golden Bears. Playing without Jake Locker, the Huskies looked to backup quarterback Carl Bonnell. Using a simplified offense focused on running the football, Washington hammered away at a dispirited Bear squad. Louis Rankin had another big day, dashing 46 yards for a touchdown on the game's first play from scrimmage. Rankin finished with 224 more yards, and the Huskies chalked up a 37-23 win.

With two games left to the regular season, Washington was now 2-6 in the Pac-10 and 4-7 overall. Games against Washington State and Hawaii remained. The topic gripping Seattle with a toxic vengeance was whether to retain Tyrone Willingham for a fourth year. A website called FireToddTurner.com cropped up and drew lots of local attention. The Husky Half Brains podcast emerged to draw attention to Willingham's job security and raise support for Jim L. Mora to succeed him. Meanwhile, the heavily-trafficked message boards at Dawgman.com were in perpetual meltdown as civil war raged on. The airwaves of sports radio KJR brimmed with boiling rhetoric from both sides. One host, Dave Grosby, took to the air each day with a hostile and dismissive tone toward all callers who said Willingham should be fired. Fellow host Mike Gastineau accused Willingham bashers of being mouth breathers and questioned their collective IQ. *Seattle Times* columnist Jerry Brewer called for calm and patience, reminding readers that Willingham had inherited one of the most difficult rebuilding jobs in college football history.

The arrival of that week's Apple Cup against Washington State was to be a special one. It marked the 100th game between the Huskies and Cougars. Boeing sponsored the festivities, including a Friday luncheon in downtown Seattle that brought the two teams together in the spirit of sportsmanship. That commitment toward sportsmanship extended into the pre-game festivities the following day. Husky and Cougar highlights were both shown on the stadium's Jumbo Tron, marking the first time that Husky Stadium had celebrated an opponent's accomplishments in this manner.

Anticipation rose as game time approached. These heated rivals each sported 4-7 records, but the winner would be crowned state champion. Fielding the opening kickoff, UW's Louis Rankin scampered all the way for a touchdown. Husky Stadium, crammed with many fans from both teams, pulsated with excitement. Jake Locker was back in the lineup and running the ball effectively. WSU quarterback Alex Brink rallied the Cougars with a brilliant offensive performance. He would shred the Husky defense for 399 yards passing, the most by any quarterback in Apple Cup history.

Brink's biggest moment of the night came with thirty-seven seconds left in the game. Coming out of a timeout, the Cougars had the ball on Washington's 35-yard line. The score was tied 35-35. The stadium pulsated with raucous anticipation. The Cougars broke huddle and approached the line of scrimmage. Looking across at the Washington defense, Brink saw the Huskies looked confused.

During the timeout, UW defensive coordinator Kent Baer had called for a blitz. But moments later, as the Huskies lined up for the play, defensive line coach Randy Hart suddenly signaled in another call for zone coverage. One of the Huskies on the field at that moment recalled the horror. "Guys were looking wide-eyed like, what? I'm looking at E.J. [Savannah] getting ready to blitz. Half the defense is running cover zero, which means there's no safety help, there's nothing back there. Everyone is man-to-man, one-on-one with someone. So if you've got your safeties blitzing and a linebacker blitzing, the cornerbacks are locked up. It's not possible to blitz and run zone at the same time unless you're in a fire zone. I was screaming 'Cover 2 carry!' at the guys. The confusion… That play was doomed from the start."

Brink took the snap and dropped straight back into the pocket. He had a blitzing defender closing in and had to hang in there tight. But he spied wide receiver Brandon Gibson breaking wide open toward the end zone. Brink laid the football up perfectly and Gibson ran underneath for the winning touchdown. The nearest Husky defender was Darrin Harris, who trailed more than ten yards behind.

"We just blew the coverage," Willingham said in the aftermath. "Communication was not good across the board." The final score: Cougars 42, Huskies 35. The loss left UW at 2-7 and last place in Pac-10 play. Overall, their record was 4-8 heading into the season finale at Hawaii. If prior speculation about Willingham's job security had been a relentless wind, it was now a raging cyclone.

Athletic director Todd Turner stood strong in the face of all swirling criticisms of Willingham, both publicly and privately. Behind the scenes, chess pieces were being moved about the proverbial board. Turner summoned Jake Locker into his office for a meeting, wanting to gauge his take on the whole situation. Prior to sitting down with Turner, Locker revealed this to a teammate.

"Jake is a great kid, a good dude," said the teammate. "He's the kind of guy that when your coach tells you something, you do it. He's not a critical thinker, he's not an extremely outside the box thinker. He's extremely funny, charismatic, a bit dorky, but the media and fans didn't get to see the real Jake. Willingham trained him to be leery of the media. Before the Hawaii game, Turner called Jake into his office. I told him that this was his chance to speak up and make a big impact for the team. And more to the point, I said 'If you tell Emmert to fire Willingham after the Hawaii game, he's gone. Tyrone would have had to find his own way back to the mainland.' But Jake didn't want anything to do with that. He said 'I don't have that kind of pull.'"

There was a bye week prior to playing the Hawaii Warriors in Honolulu. But more good news greeted the Huskies on November 30th, when coveted recruits Kavario Middleton and Jermaine Kearse announced their commitments to Washington. According to their Lakes High coach Dave Miller, both players had confidence in the direction the program was going with Willingham. Both players also said in later interviews they were going to Washington regardless of coach. Willingham supporters heralded the news as proof positive that he had the team headed in the right direction.

However, in a *Seattle Times* online poll, 69% of the fan base wanted Willingham let go after the Hawaii game, while 31% wanted him retained for the fourth year. As the team boarded the plane and took off across the Pacific Ocean toward the islands, UW players quietly celebrated. Most of them felt certain Willingham's reign at Washington was almost over.

In Hawaii, anticipation was at a fever pitch. Despite criticism of playing a weak schedule, the Warriors were nevertheless undefeated. A win over a Pac-10 conference opponent like Washington would likely secure a coveted BCS bowl berth. With star quarterback Colt Brennan and head coach June Jones, the odds seemed decent. Come the evening of December 1st, a record crowd jammed into Aloha Stadium and prepared for the party of the century. Usually overlooked by the continental United States, Hawaii football would finally receive long overdue recognition. Alas, when it started raining, the crowd went crazy, almost as if the downpour foretold a great victory was at hand.

As the game started, Jake Locker was firmly in control. He capped the opening drive with an 8-yard touchdown run. That set the tone for the first quarter. Fullback Luke Kravitz bulled across the goal line for two more scores, and with 5:23 left in the opening stanza, the Huskies led the Warriors 21-0. Washington's linemen may have been overweight, but their physical dominance over the relatively diminutive Warrior lines was evident. In the course of a few minutes, the hometown crowd had gone from a Mardi Gras frenzy to the solemnity of a funeral. Women in the stands were spotted wiping tears from their eyes as they witnessed the apparent death of a dream.

But then Colt Brennan went to work. The Hawaii quarterback dissected the Husky defense like Zorro shredding a sheet. The Huskies couldn't believe how their own best defensive lineman, Daniel Teo-Nesheim, was being held on every play. By halftime, Washington's lead was trimmed to 28-21.

With less than a minute left in the game the score was tied at 28-28. Colt Brennan hit Ryan Grice-Mullen with a 5-yard scoring strike to give Hawaii a 35-28 lead. Washington got the ball back with 38 seconds left. Locker quickly drove them to the Hawaii 4-yard line in the closing seconds. But his pass was intercepted by Warrior Ryan Mouton in the end zone, sealing the victory and Hawaii's 12-0 season.

Thousands of Warrior fans charged the field and camera flashes sparkled throughout Aloha Stadium as the islands celebrated the biggest win in school history. Washington fullback Paul Homer trudged off the field as Hawaii players and their fans began taunting him and his teammates.

"Hawaii is talking trash," recalled Homer. "Fans ran onto the field and were causing trouble. A policeman came up and I thought he was going to protect us, but he told us to get the fuck off their field. That's when you know the whole state is against you."

The scene in the locker room was the same solemn ritual. But for many of the players, the pain subsided once they returned to the team hotel. There they were, overlooking the ocean, and a feeling of relief came over them for the season was officially over. They wouldn't be returning to Seattle until the next day.

Several players including backup running back J.R Hasty were standing in the hallway talking with senior linebacker Dan Howell. At 22 years of age, Howell had been a consummate Willingham player. Always did what he was told, got good grades, was respected for having a strong character, and was exceedingly polite.

"I never do anything," Howell said. "I want to go have some fun tonight."

"You're always so straight, you got to have some fun," said Hasty, who then gave Howell a little handshake. Willingham suddenly appeared and fixed his gaze upon Howell.

"Where you going Dan?"

"I'm going out to have some fun coach," Howell said. "It's been a long season."

"Go to your room, Dan."

"Coach Willingham, please stop. What you're doing right now is ridiculous."

"Go to your room, Dan."

"I'm sorry," said Howell. "But you're not the coach anymore, you can't tell me what do. I'm going out tonight." Howell walked past him and made his way down the hallway toward the elevator. Willingham stared after him the entire way.

"Willingham sat downstairs and patrolled the lobby until the wee hours of the morning," said tight end Johnie Kirton. "We were in

Hawaii and he was trying to take away the fun of Hawaii. It was really bad, it really was. For the guys that were coming back we were excited that a new coach would be there. We had guys blatantly walking past Coach, telling him you're going to get fired, we don't play for you anymore."

Willingham had several other such confrontations. Linemen Greyson Gunheim, Jordan Reffert and Wilson Alfoa all had run-ins as they made their through the lobby and into the warm Hawaiian night. Younger players that witnessed those exchanges were bug-eyed, because these were, by-and-large, "soldiers" and "yes-men" that never rebelled against a Willingham command.

One story that spread like wildfire among the players was Willingham's encounter with senior receiver Cody Ellis. Willingham spied Ellis in a hotel hot tub with one of the Husky cheerleaders. When the coach ordered him out at once, Ellis defied him.

"I think for Willingham it was like he was muddled about the whole situation," explained Kirton. "He came to a great university and tried to build it back up, and for a man to fail on a grand scale is a blow to the heart. To this day I don't know if he blames himself or us for what happened. To us, that night at the hotel, it seemed like he wanted to catch as many people as possible and make mental notes about who was defying him. It was almost like he knew he was coming back. But that doesn't make sense when 99% of America knew he wasn't coming back."

Unbeknownst to the Washington players, a private meeting had taken place the Friday before the Hawaii game among Emmert, Turner and Willingham.

W

CHAPTER 18

Emmert's Hour of Decision

"For me to stand before you as the head coach at the University of Washington is a special opportunity and a special honor"

—Tyrone Willingham

ON the Friday prior to Washington's game with Hawaii, President Emmert entered a meeting at the Ihilani JW Marriot hotel with Todd Turner and Tyrone Willingham. Emmert went into it with a strong inclination to fire Willingham. But something occurred in that room to change his mind.

In an August 2010 interview, Emmert stated he didn't remember exactly what was said in the meeting. When asked about sources close to him who stated that Emmert planned on firing Willingham at that meeting, Emmert waved his hand in obvious irritation.

"Those conversations are obviously personal," he said. "Like everyone I wanted to know: what is the plan to make this better? Is it clear that there are solutions at hand? Tyrone had what I thought was a sensible outline to turn this around to fix things. He's a bright guy and had thought this through. Nobody was more frustrated and disappointed than him. Coaches are competitive and Tyrone is no different. He had a compelling argument he could turn this around. I found it persuasive and so did Todd."

Emmert was also aware that members of the media insisted that firing Willingham would be unfair. Columnists such as Jerry Brewer of *The Seattle Times* and KJR radio hosts Dave Grosby and Mike Gastineau voiced their opinions vociferously. A Freedom of Information request from *The Seattle Times* brought to light the many emails that deluged

Emmert from impassioned fans and people of influence. All-Pro Seahawk running back Shaun Alexander wrote: "I want to tell you how pleased I am with the direction of the program and the character of the guys Ty has been bringing in. Ty has set the table for this to happen, holding character above other things. Let him finish what he started and you'll be pleased with all your decisions."

James Bible, president of the King County chapter of the NAACP, emailed Emmert to request a meeting. "As you are likely aware, Coach Willingham has become a pillar in our community and is well on his way toward returning the football program to respectability," wrote Bible. Representatives of other black groups — the Breakfast Group and the United Black Christian Clergy of Washington State — also signaled their support of Willingham.

Former Seahawks quarterback Jeff Kemp chimed in to champion Willingham's commitment to excellence. "This man has changed lives and the reputation of UW football player culture (of which there were too many sad embarrassments before). He is building a foundation, and winning will result."

But Emmert also knew that public opinion was 69% in favor of firing Willingham—due largely to the allure and availability of Seahawk assistant Jim L Mora. Ed Hanson, a booster and former mayor of the city of Everett, offered to pay a combined $200,000 to the UW law school for the firings of Willingham and Turner. Emmert later referred to those offers as "grossly inappropriate."

Emmert was giving Mora some consideration. But the X factor in hiring him would mean firing Willingham. Private conversations at the upper campus were tinged with grave concern over the damage that a racially-charged backlash could unleash upon the university. There was the perceived risk of losing funding, and the validation of suspicions held by Seattle liberals that UW was a win-at-all-costs football factory. Their howls of protest could claim that nothing had changed since the jaundiced days of Neuheisel. Emmert had witnessed the vicious backlash that occurred to Notre Dame in December 2004 when they fired Willingham after three years, and those charges of racism still lingered. Despite his skepticism of Willingham's coaching ability, Emmert weighed both sides of the issue and reached his conclusion.

As the Washington Huskies boarded the team plane to return to the Pacific Northwest, the decision had been made to retain Willingham for the 2008 season.

Of course, none of the players knew the news. Back in Seattle, thousands of fans and regional media were on pins and needles awaiting word of Willingham's fate. They anticipated the announcement to be made by Tuesday, December 4th. But that day came and went with nary a hint. Emmert, Turner and Willingham were meeting again, going over details.

On Sports Radio KJR, Mitch Levy interviewed ESPN's Lee Corso, and began the conversation with reference to the unfolding drama.

"We've got a heck of a controversy going on out here," said Levy. "A Tyrone Willingham controversy. We're still waiting for definite word that Coach Willingham will be invited back for fourth season at Washington after finishing again dead last in the conference. What do you know of Willingham and what do you think of Willingham?"

"Well first of all I think he's a wonderful football coach," replied Corso. "But as good a football coach as he is, he's an even better human being. You're not going to get a much better person than Tyrone Willingham. I think he deserves another year at it. I know that the record is sometimes an indication of [how you're doing], but let me tell you something- the guy can coach! His staff can coach!"

Finally on December 5th, UW media relations conducted the news conference. Turner and Willingham sat down before the media as Turner announced that Willingham was returning for the 2008 season. President Emmert was not present. The conference took 37 minutes as both men proclaimed that brighter days lay ahead.

"We approached this situation as business as usual and as I always do," Turner said. "Coach Willingham and I began visiting almost immediately, even before the end of the season, talking about things that he needed that we could provide that would enable his team to have better success. As always, I involved [President Mark Emmert] in my evaluation and discussion and he had some good conversations with me and Tyrone individually and me and Tyrone together and we call came out on the same page that the building blocks are in place."

When asked about the recent recruiting gets of blue chippers

Middleton and Kearse, Turner said: "We've been really encouraged about the reception our staff has received, especially in our state. That validates the hard work and effort put in over a period of time to change perceptions of our football program here. We are creating the kind of trust and reputation that are consistent with our values, and we are starting to see the fruition of that."

Willingham, for his part, asked for fans and boosters to hang in there and be patient. "Our football team I believe is poised to do some good things. I share the disappointment that our president echoes from our boosters. No one wants to win badder than Coach Willingham and our team. I'm making the right decisions to put us in a place to win."

As the conference concluded, Willingham made his way from the room. Moments later, a cluster of athletic department employees greeted him with a rousing standing ovation.

The news swept through Western Washington and then nationwide. It served as a dagger to the heart of those in favor of a coaching change. Many season ticket holders despaired that despite its storied past, Washington no longer valued big time football. For those supporting Willingham, it was a time of righteous celebration. The media frolicked at the good news.

"It's the right move," penned John Sleeper of The Everett Herald. "The 11-25 record after three years shouldn't be the bottom line, as it is with too many of the vocal minority. The program is in better shape than it was before Willingham started – in all aspects. Too many don't remember how bad the program had become. Recruiting had become a joke. A losing mentality permeated the program. The attitude was in the toilet."

Jerry Brewer of The Seattle Times concurred. "This was neither a victory for Willingham's tame supporters nor a defeat for his ferocious detractors," he wrote. "This was simply a decision — the right decision — to delay judgment until we gain more clarity about the coach's rebuilding project. Another year should be enough time, though next season will be one of the most volatile in Huskies history. The fight didn't end with this status-quo proclamation. Really, it just began. It's on Willingham to calm the outrage with victories. His seat may be warmer now than it was even at Notre Dame. His Fighting Irish critics got the quick boot they wanted three years ago. Willingham was fired after only three seasons at a school that once was arrogant about honoring its coaching contracts. Washington's Ty bashers didn't get their way, however. So Willingham has received more of a fair shake this time. He turns 54 this month. This breathing room could either set up the final portion of his career or condemn it."

It was a measure of the fanaticism Husky fans had for the program that this controversy would carry on for several more days. KJR's Dave "Softy" Mahler went on the air and insisted that keeping Willingham was the right thing to do. He called for Husky fans to rally behind Willingham and the team. He also called out long-time booster Bill Fleenor, who had publicly stated that he wasn't investing another dime into UW athletics so long as Willingham remained. Meanwhile, Dave Samek, owner of Dawgman.com, wrote an editorial asking Husky Nation to drop the in-fighting and unify.

The other shoe dropped a week later. Word from UW was that Turner was on his way out as athletic director, effective January 31st, 2008. In comments to the press, Emmert praised Turner and said the change had nothing to do with the Willingham situation. A change was needed, he said, to serve the university's best interests. For his part, Turner made his feelings known. "The message that our students hear, that our coaches hear, that our leadership hears from the general run-of-the-mill fan is that the only thing we really care about is how many games they win. And I have to look at that after 32 years of doing this and say 'Wow, is that really what we are all about? Have I been that naïve all this period of time? I have been spending all my time on the student-athlete experience and trying to create better lives for people and the proper place in higher education when all I should have been worrying about is how many games we've won. Why didn't I go to the NFL if that's all it's about.'"

Turner, while acknowledging he had resigned, made it clear that he wasn't leaving of his own accord. "It's not so much what changed in my eyes but what changed in [Emmert's] eyes," Turner said. "I'm the same person I was when I came here."

As Turner prepared his exit from the UW athletic department, he wrote a letter to all employees. In part, it read:

> *Frankly, I've grown concerned recently over the growing imbalance between what the public (i.e. fans) expects and the true purpose of intercollegiate athletics. It's a frightening time to be in your positions if you truly believe in the ideal of the student-athlete within the framework of higher education. It will take exceedingly strong leadership to hold us true to this ideal. In recent days, I've seen a side of athletics that sickens me with the incessant interloping of uninformed, unenlightened, self-anointed experts who look upon intercollegiate athletics solely as entertainment to satisfy their own self interests. That's why competitive success at the UW without compromising values, character, and integrity is so essential. Someone has to be the example. It might as well be the Huskies.*

W

Husky fan Scott Liljedahl sent 10th place trophies to President Emmert, Todd Turner and Tyrone Willingham

CHAPTER 19

Mitchie the Kid's Rant

In the days following the announcement that Tyrone Willingham would be retained for the 2008 season, many sports fans throughout the Puget Sound region rejoiced and vehemently defended the decision. Among those stupefied by this was radio host Mitch Levy of 950 KJR Sports Radio. Levy, who hails from New York and possesses no allegiance to the UW, expressed his bewilderment during an on-air rant on December 7, 2007.

SO I've been driving around and listening to the radio station and reading my emails and reading the blogs and reading the letters to the editor in the last thirty-six hours since this Tyrone Willingham thing broke that he's coming back. I've heard a few of the radio hosts here at the station and everyone's got a different viewpoint and it's what makes the world go around and its fine.

But I've got to tell ya... I just have to stop and say a few things. Either I am naïve or I am just misguided. Because I thought all along that he would probably be retained. As you know, my feeling is I wouldn't retain him at the expense of losing Mora but outside of Mora I would give a fourth shot even though he's done a lousy job—I didn't think there was any question he's done a lousy job. And I thought the debate, once we got to this point, we all agree that the first three years have been lousy, now does he deserve a fourth year because of the extenuating circumstances of the program? And does he deserve another shot because of what's going on around the program and continuity—I thought that would be the debate.

I didn't realize, and call me naïve, that I was going to sit around thirty-six hours after this thing, and actually listen to Husky fans, a HUGE chunk of fans, actually try to convince me that the first three years of the Tyrone Willingham administration has been a success

I've got to tell you. I've been driving around listening to this stuff, hosts on this station, callers of this station, Husky fans, I am in absolute disbelief how many different people have tried to fool themselves into believing that a team that has won less Pac-10 games than Stanford... Three years ago, when Tyrone Willingham took over this program, if you would have polled college football experts around the country and the question would have been this: What is the worst BCS program in America? Where is it the most difficult to win BCS games of any BCS conference team in America, I'm not sure Stanford would have won it, but they would have been in the conversation three years ago. And three years later, Washington has won less Pac-10 games than Stanford. They have finished last, second-to-last and last [in the Pac-10]. And I am sitting around for 36 hours listening to caller after caller, some of the hosts, I'm listening to people try to literally rationalize... Oh the air of the program... It's not important how many games he wins... It's not important how many bowls they haven't gone to... It's not important that he can't make halftime adjustments and he gets outcoached in games... It's not important that they're disorganized at the end of games... It's not important that 5 guys are playing zone and 6 guys are blitzing in the most important play of the Apple Cup... It's not that they're eliminated mathematically from going to a bowl game three games to go in the season...

What's important is that there's an air about the program... He's brought discipline and the kids are enjoying the college experience...

I'm sitting back here listening to this... and listening to all these Husky fans and this is what I've been thinking and you tell me whether I'm wrong on this: Can you imagine if football fans from Auburn, or football fans from Alabama, or football fans from Florida State or Miami or Ohio State or Michigan or Penn State were eavesdropping on the last 36 hours of this radio station?

What would hardcore fans from these prestigious football programs, what would they be saying? If they were listening to guys, one after the other, call a radio station and claim that the head coach has done a good job not because they finished last, second-to-last and last in the conference, he's brought discipline.... I got a call yesterday on my voice mail. "You should see how many people are volunteering to work out in the off-season workout program, Mitch."

It's not about the fact that they're disorganized at the end of games and he has to call time outs before critical two point conversions and he can't get plays off. It's not about the fact that they're losing 48-41 to a lowly Arizona team at home and giving up 700 yards. "The program is thriving Mitch because there's this improved air."

Washington fans would be the laughing stock of the country if people heard this around the country. If real football fans heard this, heard the chatter that's been on this station. I've told you this before: I believe that Tyrone Willingham in a private moment would tell you he's done a lousy job over the last three years. I can't believe we're debating... There's literally a chunk of Husky Nation that believe for alternative cockamamie reasons that Tyrone Willingham at 6-20 in the conference and worse than Stanford by two games in that span, has done a good job. And I know that sometimes we talk about sports fans in Chicago, sports fans in Philadelphia, sports fans in New York, sports fans in Boston... and I'm not suggesting to you that because Philadelphia sports fans boo Santa Claus or Chicago sports fans throw batteries at guys, that that's necessarily a better sports fan than Seattle sports fans. But I've got to say this morning... To the group of Washington fans, and you know who you are, that are actually rationalizing what's happened over the three years as a good performance, finding cockamamie ways to claim he's done a good job over the three years, could you get a little red ass in you? Just a little bit? Stop being pansies! Stop being wussies! I hate to sound like Dan Hawkins of the University of Colorado, but THIS IS A FOOTBALL TEAM! HE'S A FOOTBALL COACH! Stop coming up with these alternative ways to try to rationalize that the guy has done a good job over three years because of these vague kind of positives about the program. It makes fans of the University of Washington sound like wussies. TOUGHEN UP! Demand some excellence from a win-loss perspective... Could you imagine if the University of Alabama sunk, because everything is cyclical, had a bad stretch and sunk to the level of the Washington program, and then for three years straight, won a total of six games in the SEC and won two games less than Ole Miss in a three year period, do you think people in Alabama and Tuscaloosa would be calling and going "Ohhhh, but the coach is doing a good job because there's discipline and guys are in offseason workouts and they love playing for the coach..." Do you think anybody is Tuscaloosa, Alabama would even think of calling a show and saying here are some alternative reasons why the guy has done a good job and it's not about wins and losses? It's pathetic. It's laughable and pathetic.

W

UW President Mark Emmert watches Husky defense collapse in the final moments of the 2007 Apple Cup

CHAPTER 20

Emmert Reflects

"Given the information we had available and what I saw in front of me last year, we made the right choice."

—UW President Mark Emmert, on whether he regretted bringing back Tyrone Willingham for the 2008 season

ON an overcast afternoon in August 2010, in the waning days of his presidency at the University of Washington, Mark Emmert prepared to assume the presidency of the NCAA. But for the moment, he sat down with a visitor and reflected on the Tyrone Willingham debacle at Washington.

"First of all, everyone recognizes that Tyrone is just an extraordinary guy," Emmert said. "He handles himself very well. He's someone who is a very good role model for student athletes. He cares about the students as students. All of those things were very compelling. He started to bring to bear his values and style to a program that had really suffered a lot. We weren't having off the field problems and we weren't having academic problems. He was getting kids to perform well in pretty much every aspect in their lives, and that was important to us. I would see him a number of times each year. We would talk football of course, but we would talk about other things. He has a delightful family and a wonderful wife and he enjoyed all that. One of the pleasant things about Tyrone is that he's an interesting guy and likes to talk about a variety of subjects. And that makes him fun and interesting."

However, fun and interesting were not proper words describing Husky Football during the 2007 Apple Cup. In the final seconds,

Emmert stood in the back of the end zone at Husky Stadium and watched the carnage play out before him. Cougar wide receiver Brandon Gibson, breaking free from confused Husky pass coverage, ran straight at Emmert with no defender within fifteen yards of him. Gibson hauled in the easy pass from quarterback Alex Brink, and Washington State secured the win. The dejected Husky players trudged back to the bench beneath a cascade of boos from stunned and angered fans.

Neither did Emmert escape the fans' wrath. After all, as president of the university, he had final say over personnel decisions. Bill Gates Sr., head of the Board of Regents, applied no pressure upon him, but many fans and boosters expressed their outrage. Some sent ugly emails while others shouted insults. Walking with his wife near the stands after the Apple Cup, a fan shouted an obscenity at him. The couple kept walking but Mrs. Emmert leaned toward her husband and expressed her disapproval. Emmert shrugged and told her if he was in the stands he would be yelling it too.

"I understood their frustration," Emmert said. "I'm a Husky, I was frustrated. Tyrone was frustrated. Everyone knew this was going badly. Everyone felt bad about it."

Back in November 2006, when the "Suddenly Senior" situation boiled over as Willingham took away the senior seasons of a handful of Husky players, Emmert's antennae went up enough that he inquired with his athletic director. "Every coach in every sport has to make decisions who is going to be part of the team and who they will offer scholarships to," he said. "[As president] I worry about several things. One, that young people will be treated fairly and that the University of Washington is consistent with its commitments. And secondly, that we're following all of our rules. I talked to Todd and felt comfortable with his answers that Tyrone was being fair with these kids and was consistent with the rules and good for the program in the long run. Obviously, some of those athletes felt differently about that decision but ultimately I have to let coaches make those decisions."

Despite Emmert's assertions that Willingham was being fair to the players, people within the athletic department and the coaching staff knew differently. By the time of "Suddenly Senior", those around Willingham saw that he had a chip on his shoulder and a sense of entitlement. His staff knew he didn't have a handle on how to motivate and inspire players. That he didn't foster the love and care of teammates for each other. And that his petty and capricious punishments made players doubt themselves and damaged team morale.

"I wasn't aware of it of course," Emmert said. "The culture inside the football team is impossible for a university president to judge. It's one of the challenges for a president that you're always judging things from the edge and not from inside. At the time I was reassured that those were decisions that made sense and were consistent with the behavior of the program so I didn't intervene in them."

Toward the end of the 2007 season, Emmert sensed that communication breakdowns might be occurring between players and coaches.

"The only way it surfaced to me was in watching the dynamics," Emmert said. "It's not so much what's happening on the scoreboard, but the responsiveness you see from young people in the demeanor and their behavior and the manner they are practicing and playing and how they are feeling about their experience. When we bring a young person to the university, it's up to us to provide all the resources that they need to be successful at the highest level they are capable. It doesn't matter whether it's physics or football. You recruit the smartest, most capable and talented kids you can. You bring them to the university with a promise that you're going to allow them to succeed. And then I have to take responsibility too for putting the best professors, staff, equipment and facilities that we can afford in front of those people, and create a culture that supports a very high level of performance.

"What was troubling to me was that after a number of years we were failing to do that. You read between the lines with body language and behavior. I talked with Todd a lot and relied on his judgment."

As the 2007 season concluded, Emmert, Turner and Willingham met privately in the team hotel in Hawaii, the day before season finale against the Warriors. Exactly what took place in that room is a mystery, but Emmert confided to those close to him that he entered the meeting with the intention of firing Willingham. Two years and nine months after the fact, Emmert couldn't recall any details of what was said in the meeting. But he remembered that both he and Turner left the meeting impressed with the plan Willingham had proposed to turn the program's future around.

"I went back to 'why do we play this game?'" said Emmert. "'What are we trying to achieve here? What's the purpose?' I got back to, 'this is all about these young people, and providing them an opportunity to fulfill their capacity as students and as athletes.' And were we or weren't we doing it? The performance on the field would indicate we weren't getting that done… I was talking regularly with Todd. We were having conversations about how tough it was and how to turn it around."

After Washington's crushing defeat to Hawaii, the team returned to Seattle. In the days that followed, Willingham was retained and the public uproar – both pro and con—railed throughout Western Washington. But a week later came Emmert's firing of Turner – a move catching many by surprise.

"I liked Todd a lot and he has many things about him I admire a lot," recalled Emmert. "He's a good man. Making that decision was very hard. We have expectations that we will be excellent in everything we do. I didn't have confidence that he was the right leader at that time to allow our athletes to compete at the highest level they could."

Turner wasn't so magnanimous in his public comments referring to Emmert. Turner despised the emphasis on winning, and accused Emmert of placing winning over values of scholastic achievement and the so-called student experience.

"There's a criticism you'll hear from people that at the end of the day all the president and everyone else cared about was winning," said Emmert. "Of course its nonsensical in one sense. But to say you care about winning is not a bad thing. Being competitive ought to be one of the core values of a program. I want our math department to produce mathematicians that go out and win all the competitions they enter, which they do all the time by the way. They're really good at it and they're really proud of the fact that they're good competitors. But you do want your athletic programs to be competitive. Heck yes we're going to compete. Heck yes we're going to try to win championships. It's not all of what it's about, but it's part of it. When we bring in athletes, it's with the commitment and tacit promise that we're going to allow them to compete for championships. So when we're not doing that we're failing them."

When asked about the rumors that the NAACP influenced his decision, Emmert was resolute. "Absolutely not. I know that's a popular theory out there, but it really did not. It was a decision using my best judgment on what was the right and fair thing to do there."

As the discussion came to an end, Emmert was asked his overall summation of Willingham's woeful time at Washington. "The disappointment is the lack of success we had," he said. "I've never had a coach I've wanted to succeed more than Ty because I like him so much. So to not have that work out and not be able to fix that was disappointing. The most important thing is to remember the context. Tyrone inherited a program in great disarray. The program was coming off the turmoil of Rick Neuheisel's era, and the sudden shift to a new interim coach. You had players recruited by one coach and coached by two others. He had a tough hand dealt to him. He also had a tough schedule [in 2007 & 2008] which we both inherited. I'm just sad it didn't work out."

Senior Johnie Kirton introduced for his final home game in 2008

CHAPTER 21

Apocalypse

"It just seems to me to be time to quit the whining and accept it. Willingham's got at least another year. Deal with it. The program is in better shape than it was when he started here. Deal with that, too."

—John Sleeper, Columnist,
Everett Herald, December 2007

DECEMBER 5, 2007 was a day Johnie Kirton will never forget. The 6'3" 280 pound senior-to-be was hanging out with teammates watching TV, when breaking news came across the bottom of the screen. WILLINGHAM TO RETURN TO UW FOR 2008 SEASON. Everyone's jaw dropped and the room went silent in horror. Then the guys started yelling and cursing as cell phones rang like crazy. "We were all sitting there going, 'ARE YOU FUCKING KIDDING ME? WE HAVE TO PUT UP WITH THIS GUY FOR ANOTHER YEAR?'" Kirton recalled. "Guys immediately started wondering if they should transfer or quit football. Guys did not want Willingham around. But guys like me and Juan Garcia and Walt Winter had decided that we were going to stick it out no matter who the coach was.

"Every day for the next several weeks we would see each other and we always repeated the same thing day after day. CAN YOU BELIEVE THIS IS HAPPENING? HOW COULD EMMERT AND TURNER BRING HIM BACK? The younger guys didn't know what to expect, because they hadn't endured what we had endured for the past three years. We knew what to expect.

"A few of us caught wind that he played the race card; that he brought up the NAACP as leverage. I don't think it was too far from something that Willingham would do, to try to hold onto the last string to stay as coach at Washington. All of us were always asking: Why is he trying to hold on? He seemed like he was going to accept fate, but then changed his mind and refused to back down from anything which is a good trait, but why would he come back to a place where he was not wanted? To come back for the last year, he caused a lot of pain."

As December turned to January, media support remained sympathetic to Willingham. When off-season conditioning drills got underway, Dawgman.com columnist Dick Baird painted an optimistic portrait. "Coach Willingham is one of the most respected men in the profession of coaching," wrote Baird. "If it works out like I want it to, then he will be the Husky football coach for 15 more years and retire as one of the greatest coaches in the history of the school and the conference. Remember everyone was after Don [James'] job during the first three years at Washington. The guy is a good person and is well respected by the kids on the team and as far as I'm concerned they have the first vote."

Ironically, players were voting about Willingham that January, but the proceedings were shrouded in fear and secrecy. Between 30-35 players held clandestine meetings in the locker room, outside the locker room, and in players' apartments. They organized a petition to take to President Emmert which carried the threat of a boycott unless Willingham was fired immediately. However, what terrified the players was the possibility that Emmert would decline, and then Willingham would know who planned the coup. The consensus formed that the movement needed Jake Locker's involvement. With the golden boy leading the way, the players felt Emmert couldn't possibly say no. But again, Locker wanted no part of this insurrection. Everyone was too afraid to take the lead and speak out.

At the end of that month, Ken Armstrong and Nick Perry of *The Seattle Times* made national news with a series of articles called *Victory and Ruins.* They wrote a scathing depiction of lawlessness by Washington's 2000 Rose Bowl season under former coach Rick Neuheisel. Its primary focus was on four members of that team. The criminal exploits of Jerramy Stevens, Jeremiah Pharms and the late Curtis Williams were delved into with great detail. The final feature was on linebacker Anthony Kelley, who had emerged from the ghetto and was now pursuing his Masters Degree from UW. "I was the token black guy," Kelley recalled. "That was good PR for the Seattle Times. When I realized how big this story was in the beginning, with Neuheisel and Barbara Hedges, I was the token black guy at the university. We've got all these bad stories going on, but HEY! WE'VE GOT A BLACK FOOTBALL PLAYER DOING WELL. THIS IS SOME BIG SHIT HERE! This isn't it a white tennis player. He's a black football player with a poor academic history coming from a broken home and issues including ADD. I was the poster child for all minorities in the standard. I was held as the exception to the rule."

Part of the Times' feature on Kelley described the educational trips he led to South Africa. Kelley's own trip there in 2002 had changed his life. Now he was organizing and leading other UW athletes on the same journey. The article seethed at how Neuheisel and his coaching staff had tried to dissuade Kelley from going on that 2002 trip, but implied now that with Willingham at UW, the program was being cleaned up and the focus on academic development was back where it needed to be.

Around the same time that that article came out, Johnie Kirton sat in Willingham's office having a meeting with his coach. "I had been approached Anthony Kelley about studying abroad. I wanted to follow him there because he became a mentor to me. But when Willingham heard that me and Luke Kravitz were planning on going to South Africa, he threatened to take away our scholarships. 2008 was our senior year, and I promised Willingham to come back in even better shape. Anthony put his neck on the line for us. It came down to him talking to every president of the school board at the university. He went to bat for us, talked to Emmert. I don't want to blame Willingham, but he sold us a false dream. In that meeting he told me that he needed defensive linemen. He knew I had been a running back and tight end. Not to toot my own horn, but I was always a team guy. He said take your time to make a decision. I prayed on it and talked to my family about it and then told Willingham I was willing to make the switch."

Kirton and Kravitz spent the time studying in South Africa. For Kirton, the experience was everything he hoped it would be and more. He fulfilled his promise and worked out hard that summer, arriving at 2008 fall camp in good shape. He noticed a profound change in Willingham's demeanor. "He was a completely different person. He was no longer the Willingham third person prick. He had this vibe about him that was really bad. His words were empty, but there was this bitterness. I found out that Willingham had promised those incoming true freshmen that they would be starting on the line if they signed with him. So now on top of everything, he had taken away my NFL dream. That was the biggest blow to me; not only had I never lost so many games in my life, but I made a huge goal of going overseas and fulfilled it, but now I was punished for making the life-changing decision. Willingham had always said to build yourself up and become a great man, and I had bought into it, and then was scolded and punished for developing myself. That fall camp was just a feeling of loathing. Of being punished. Seeing true freshmen who had never taken a class being made starters in front of me. Luke lost his desire to play football at all. To see a guy like Luke put so much time and effort into a program, and then see it all stepped on, was sad to see."

Kirton wasn't the only one noticing Willingham's bitter vibe. The coach's relationship with the press, always detached and cryptic, had mutated into hostility. Bob Condotta of *The Seattle Times* caught the full brunt. One day during fall camp, an athletic department official came to him saying Willingham wanted to speak with him in private. When he encountered Willingham, the coach held a clipboard containing Condotta's article that day. Certain sections were highlighted. Without giving eye contact, Willingham read the offensive sections. He said he didn't like his use of sources. When finished, he informed Condotta that he would not talk to him the rest of the season.

For the next ten days or so, the same scene repeated itself at each daily briefing. Condotta would ask a question, and Willingham either stared at him in silence or else looked away and said "next question." Condotta's boss at the newspaper told him to keep pressing the issue.

But after about ten days Condotta stopped beating his head against this brick wall.

Dawgman.com's Chris Fetters would soon have his own run-in with Willingham. For several weeks, a shroud of mystery surrounded linebacker E.J. Savannah. Willingham had inexplicably told reporters that Savannah was academically ineligible even though his grades were up to par. The linebacker also suffered an off-season injury and reporters were trying to uncover whether he was going to play. No one had seen him at camp.

During a briefing, Fetters asked for an update on Savannah. At first, Willingham mysteriously acted like he had no idea who Savannah was. As Fetters pressed, Willingham became openly perturbed and refused to answer the question. "Do you see him here?" the coach asked. "Then your eyes are as good as mine." The gaffe made by Willingham was that a UW camera was on him and broadcast that exchange onto the internet. Within a day, the video had been seen by several hundred people. For some, it was the first time they had glimpsed the dark side to Willingham's personality.

But the Husky players knew that side of Willingham all too well and forwarded the link around. They gathered around computers watching with glee and forwarding the link around. "We all saw the Fetters YouTube video," said a player. "Willingham never should have kicked E.J. off the team to begin with. Willingham had him undergo a series of drug tests and he passed all of them. That was the condition to coming back. He did everything Tyrone told him to do and he still wouldn't let him get back on the team."

For Willingham's part, he refused to give any reason to anyone, including Savannah himself, who saw his junior season slip away to Willingham's whim. "The parties involved know what they are," said Willingham. "Sometimes those things can change overnight. Sometimes they may be forever."

It seemed no one within close range could escape the coach's wrath that fall camp—even fans. 31-year old James Cornell, a rabid Husky fan and the nephew of former UW fullback Bo Cornell, found himself banned from practice. Being a Tyee member and huge Willingham fan, Cornell had jumped through the necessary hoops with the athletic department to be able to attend practice with his father. After doing so, he wrote an innocuous post on the premium message board of Dawgman.com. He jokingly sneered at the posters who wanted Willingham fired, saying that the team was working hard and looking great.

Willingham, who frequently read newspapers, websites and message boards where discussions on Husky football prevailed, was livid. A call came from the athletic department that Cornell and his dad were banned from all practices. Cornell was still in a state of shock when he fielded another call.

"Jennifer Cohen, a really nice lady from the athletic department, called me," recalled Cornell. "She apologized for Willingham's behavior and said things had been tense around there. She offered to take me out to lunch to smooth things over and that she appreciated our support of the program. But she said that at this time it's up to Willingham to let you back into practice. I don't think I did anything wrong. I defended the guy and said the players were giving great effort. I thought Willingham's reaction was ridiculous. Maybe it was blind faith just wanting to see him be successful. I had subscribed to the fact that the players were young and that Neuheisel had destroyed the program. I think I was in denial. I didn't want to believe that we were going to have to go through all this again. I would listen to Softy Mahler and Dick Baird and Hugh Millen on the Husky Honks on KJR and they would talk about needing 3-4 years to turn a program around. So I would think okay, Willingham needs one more year. Let's give him one more year."

Despite the boiling inner turmoil, many Husky fans had minimal awareness of its existence. Anticipation for the season opener was building to a fever pitch. Washington was traveling to Eugene to go against 20th ranked Oregon. The game had the entire Northwest abuzz. Jake Locker, now a sophomore, assuredly gave the Huskies some hope. The Ducks, led by quarterback Dennis Dixon, held lofty aspirations for a monster season.

A record crowd jammed into Autzen Stadium for the August 30th matchup. Both teams ran onto the field under the bright lights and electrified atmosphere. As Washington's offense went out for its first series, the visual discrepancy between the two teams startled anyone there to witness it. Washington guard Casey Bulyca, when lining up against the Ducks, felt a surge of anger toward Willingham and trainer Trent Greener. Here were the Huskies linemen, with pipe cleaner arms and beer guts, going against the Oregon players, who were ripped and defined.

By some sort of miracle, the Huskies weren't getting blown out, not at first. When UW fullback Paul Homer got stuffed at the goal line, it set up a fourth and goal situation. Washington called time out and Jake Locker jogged over and pleaded with offensive coordinator Tim Lappano to go with Homer again. Lappano relented, and on the following play, Homer took the ball off tackle and into the end zone. As a Duck defender grabbed Homer by the legs and tried to pull him backwards. Locker intervened, pushing the opposing player away and shouting "He's in, bitch!" This cut Oregon's lead to 14-10.

But the second half was when the dam burst, as was so typical in the Willingham era. The Ducks outscored the Huskies 30-0 in the third and fourth quarters, to win the game 44-10. The derisive laughter and mocking coming from the Oregon fans was surreal, but the Huskies had to stand there and take it. Up in the visitor's suite, athletic director Scott Woodward was swearing furiously.

Johnie Kirton, now embarking on his senior season, mostly watched that Oregon game from the sideline. As requested, he had made the switch to the defensive line, but it was all for naught. Pure freshmen were starting on the line, just as Willingham had promised them. "It was my senior year. I had made a huge position change. It was a bad feeling, unfortunately. Now, I was turning over the old coals... should I have transferred back in 2005? Should I have never signed with Washington?

"Coming out of high school, I made a signing day decision to not sign with Oregon and go with Washington. I was so passionate about beating Oregon, because I felt like I should have been there. Just to show Coach Campbell and Coach Bellotti that I didn't make a mistake. The last two times I played them, I cried. I was more mad at myself than anything. It was those reoccurring thoughts.

"I was a senior who had put in my blood, sweat and tears, and then for the lineup against Oregon we've got freshmen in there starting and they were shaking in their boots to be going against one of the best teams in the Pac-10."

Following a heartbreaking home loss to BYU, the Huskies were 0-2, with the powerhouse Oklahoma Sooners coming to Seattle with Heisman Trophy Candidate Sam Branford at quarterback. In years past, a screaming sellout crowd would have been a given. But several thousand seats remained empty this year.

During pre-game warm-ups, a group of Husky players were walking down the tunnel on their way to the field, when up they saw a group of Sooner players blocking the way. The Oklahoma contingent boxed the Huskies in, taunting them with threats of physical abuse, and herded the Huskies back up the tunnel. The Washington players knew that fighting back could mean a permanent trip to the Willingham doghouse, so they didn't dare to do anything. A few minutes later, while the entire Husky squad was in the team room, the door flung open and a handful of Sooner players entered and strutted to the front of the room. Again, they openly taunted the Washington players. When they left, a couple Huskies shouted they were going to pay Oklahoma back for that insult. Willingham ordered them to refrain from any retaliation. "Gentlemen," he said, "we will let our play do our talking for us on the field.'

"At alumni BBQs, the players from the Don James years would tell us stories how they would cut the lights in the tunnel and fight with the other team to intimidate them," said Kirton. "But now we had a Big 12 team trying to intimidate us. It was kind of sad. Some of our guys were fired up after that, but Coach Willingham said there will be none of that coming from us. It had a crushing effect to our spirit. Nobody before ever came into the Dawghouse and bullied us. When Willingham first came to Washington he said that a Dawg was a vicious animal. But that Oklahoma thing, that sucked the life out of us. Even the fresh meat guys who were out there playing saw that happen, and it crushed their sense that we could be a top 10 team."

Once the game started, Washington never stood a chance. With seconds left in the first half, Oklahoma led 34-0. The Huskies had the ball inside the Sooner 2 yard line, and Willingham inexplicably sent out the field goal unit. Of course, the kick was botched. Fans were booing and the whole scene at Husky Stadium was a disaster. By game's end, Bradford had completed 18 of 21 passes for 304 yards and 5 touchdowns, as Oklahoma cruised 55-14.

The next week was another home loss, this time to Stanford. Jake Locker, while blocking downfield, broke his thumb and was lost for the season. Seven days later, the Huskies traveled to Tucson to play the Arizona Wildcats. Another day, another defeat, this time to the tune of 48-14. Senior offensive lineman Casey Bulyca, at 330 pounds, was beset by a knee injury. Doctors drained fluid from his knee, which had ballooned to the size of a beach ball. Two days later, he had surgery. When he awoke, his parents informed him that the doctor said he couldn't play football ever again. "I didn't even get a phone call from Willingham, the guy I had sacrificed and played for all those years," said Bulyca. "I'm out there busting my ass and getting shot up with drugs to play football for this team, and did he come to the hospital? Not a chance. It just broke my heart. It was like getting kicked in the nuts."

A second overthrow was plotted, but it too was doomed to failure. "I tried to get guys to organize a coup on Tyrone," said Bulyca. "The wheels had fallen off. All his fancy words and bullshit freshmen running around doing whatever they wanted. I was at a loss. What is going on? Why did I get punished for cursing in public, and yet these guys who have barely been on campus are getting away with murder? These guys are not going to class or workouts, but starting in the games on Saturday. And this is the kind of shit you're going to allow to happen?"

By October 18th, when Oregon State came to Husky Stadium, a suffocating despair hung like a death pall over the entirety of Husky football. Athletic director Scott Woodward reaffirmed his position that Willingham's job performance would not be evaluated until season's end. Public pressure was enormous for a firing. The fans that had defended Willingham tooth and claw the previous December were nowhere to be seen. And another beat down was now in store, administered by the Beavers to the tune of 34-13. Washington's record was 0-6.

With Notre Dame coming to town, an odd feeling of things coming full circle was in the air. Willingham's old team, struggling mightily under the guidance of Coach Charlie Weis, would square off one final time against his current team.

Willingham was cracking under the pressure. At a 7:30 AM team breakfast at a downtown Seattle hotel, some players were talking and broke out in laughter. Willingham stood up and slammed his silverware down, spilling grape juice all over the suit and tie of assistant coach Mike Denbrock. "We felt it made him look like a fool," said Kirton. "But we knew it was because he was on the hot seat."

Kirton saw his senior season frittering away, as he was only playing sporadically. Football held little meaning for him anymore, and daily life was arduous. "By the Notre Dame game, we're 0-6," said Kirton. "We were thinking wow, how did it get to this point? I started seeing the young guys no longer care. Several starters were freshmen and sophomores, and we were getting blown out in every game. And why? Oh that's right, you're letting my senior year go to waste because you made promises to high school students that if they signed at Washington you would make them a starter. It was one of only two times that I broke down in college. I called my dad and told him: *I need you more than ever to keep me grounded and motivated, because football is no longer what I ever thought it would be.* I had my handful of teammates that were going to stick it out no matter what, and yet all these underclassmen were out there. We had no power of word, we had nothing. It was a disaster."

The players were again wondering why Emmert and the administration had given Willingham a fourth year. "It had become comfortable to lose, and that's not a good thing at all," Kirton said. "You've given him a fourth year. We had a team there back in 2006 that should have won at least 8-9 games, but we had the wrong guy coaching us. We already had the pieces in place to succeed, but there was all the talk about needing to rebuild."

But nothing was being built. Everything was being torn down. Willingham's surly manner worsened with each week. Athletic department employees, including Scott Woodward, apologized profusely to the players on a daily basis.

To long time observers of college football watching the Washington-Notre Dame game, it was unbelievable seeing thousands of empty seats throughout Husky Stadium. As Jake Locker, dressed in street clothes, continued to watch helplessly from the sideline, the Huskies were overwhelmed by another opponent. By halftime, the Fighting Irish led 17-0 and had outgained Washington 238-38 in total yardage. UW's backup quarterback Ronnie Fouch mustered a mere 5 yards passing in the first half. By the end of the day, Notre Dame left Seattle having won 33-7. Washington was now 0-7.

The glory and legacy of Washington football was now destroyed. For anyone within the program's orbit, the pressure and sadness felt unbearable. Tyrone Willingham's record at Washington stood at 11-32. He was the only coach in UW history to have four consecutive losing seasons. The three worst defenses in Husky history belonged to Willingham. The following Monday, Woodward summoned Willingham to his office to inform him he was being fired. Willingham took the news badly, becoming very upset and emotional. Woodward heard him out and then thanked him for his service. But Woodward explained that he and President Emmert had made the decision and it was final.

Willingham, with one year remaining on his contract, would receive a $1 million buyout at season's end. At Woodward's request, he would also remain as head coach until the season was finished.

At noon on Monday, Woodward and Willingham sat together before the media and made the announcement. Woodward said the search for a new coach would begin immediately. Willingham indicated that he didn't have any desire to quit. "It's just not in my makeup," he said.

In speaking with the *Seattle PI*, President Emmert said "discreet inquiries" had already been made in their search for the next Husky coach. He and Woodward would be aggressively combing the country for the best candidate.

For Johnie Kirton and the Washington Huskies, the miserable beat marched on. Next up was a trip to Los Angeles to take on powerhouse USC, led by Coach Pete Carroll and offensive coordinator Steve Sarkisian. Washington trudged onto the field with no life and long faces. As the opening kickoff sailed through the air, the beat down commenced. The Trojans tallied touchdowns on their first six possessions to lead 42-0 at the half. They played subs in the second and cruised to a 56-0 win. It was Washington's worst loss since 1929. Only a handful of Huskies showed effort. "I was embarrassed to be playing with a lot of the guys on the team that day," Kirton said. "A lot of guys quit. I was talking to my teammates throughout the game. USC is USC, they're a big time school like we used to be. But it wasn't registering with them. They didn't care."

Throughout the contest, the Trojans toyed with and taunted the Huskies. They called them pussies, faggots, and the like. Washington offered neither effort nor resistance.

"I felt like shit, I felt awful," said fullback Paul Homer. "My goal was no longer focused on getting everyone else up. My goal was to show that I was a man and that I was one of the Huskies that still had some dignity. I saw guys quitting. I have played sports my whole life, baseball, football, basketball and soccer. I've seen bad players and I've been on bad teams in my life. But I've never seen guys just quit. That was tough to see so many guys quit. It hurt me a lot. It hurt a lot of guys on the team. It will take me a long time to forgive some of those guys."

Following a 39-19 loss to Arizona State, the Huskies (now at 0-9) prepared to host UCLA for the final home game of the season on November 15th. This one came with an odd twist: former UW coach Rick Neuheisel would be coming back to Seattle, as he was in his first year as UCLA's head coach.

"It was the last home game for seniors," Kirton said. "I thought about the all the older guys going back many decades, about how they always had a fire about them and about what U-Dub meant to them. The night before the game I made a sleeveless white t-shirt that said DAWG 4 LIFE, and THANK YOU. I was going to wear it. The hardest part was like I felt I failed my university. Not only did we lose a lot of games, we were going down in history as one of the worst teams in college football history.

"Before the game, I put the shirt on," continued Kirton. "Willingham pulls me aside and says 'You're not going out there with that shirt on.' I gave him the yes sir. But I was thinking *you're crazy if you think I am going to listen to you at this point.*"

As the team exited the tunnel, they formed a line through which the seniors would be introduced one-by-one. At the last moment, Kirton pulled the giant white shirt on over his shoulder pads.

"I run through the line of teammates, and Willingham sees me coming closer and closer," Kirton said. "The look on his face is like THIS SON OF A BITCH IS REALLY GOING TO DEFY ME. As I shook his hand, I felt no bitterness or remorse. But you could cut his tension with a knife. But it was like that final sentence of a book. It was like he didn't want to be here for us or for the U-Dub. The audacity of telling me not to wear a shirt that says Dawg 4 Life."

What stood out for senior lineman Casey Bulyca, hobbling out of the tunnel on crutches, were the empty seats and the sadness in the stadium. "I stuck it out for that long, I figured I might as well get introduced even while on one leg. Being a Husky was all I wanted to do since I was a little boy. I was emotional about it since I couldn't go out the way I wanted. I gave Coach Neuheisel a hug before the game. It was a real sad experience, because he was the one that first recruited me to Washington."

Prior to kickoff, the look on Neuheisel's face as he looked into the grandstands of Husky Stadium was one of stunned exasperation. Long gone were the days when he roamed those sidelines before crowds of 70,000. Despite this game's announced crowd of 59,738, there were maybe 25,000 fans in attendance.

UCLA was a dreadful team, having won only three games that year. But they would head back to Los Angeles with their fourth, having trounced Washington 27-7.

On November 19th, amid the bitter cold and darkness, forty people gathered at the mouth of an upscale neighborhood in Kirkland. Word was that Jim L. Mora always left extremely early for Seahawks headquarters. The gathering group didn't want to take any chances of missing him. Even though Mora was slated to become the Seahawks head coach in 2009, these fans wanted to let him know he was wanted, especially on his birthday.

The group's leaders were Craig Robinson and Joel Koppenaal, who had created the website HireJimMora.com back in September. Their goal was to draw attention to Jim L Mora as well as to poke fun at the absurdity of giving Willingham the fourth year. It didn't take long for the website to take off. Several media outlets drew attention to it and numerous Husky fans emailed them looking to see how they could get involved.

A few days prior, KJR's Dave "Softy" Mahler emailed Robinson asking him to rally the troops to gather and greet Mora on his birthday. Robinson sent out a call to arms, via his website and on the message boards of Dawgman.com. When the group assembled, they were wearing Husky gear and carrying signs and banners. The clincher was Softy, who arrived with the event's centerpiece: a birthday cake with the inscription HAPPY BIRTHDAY JIM! The group flanked the road and waited. Roughly an hour passed and others from his neighborhood started leaving for work. Some stopped their cars to chat with the group, while others honked as they drove by. After ninety minutes, there had been no sign of Mora. A scouting party was dispatched to Mora's house to see if he was awake or if they had missed home. They came back and reported that he was still home. So the wait continued, and members of the group began calling in late to work.

Around 7 AM, a reporter from KOMO news radio suddenly showed up. Dave "Softy" Mahler ducked out of sight and the rest debated what to do. The project was intended to be a stealth mission. The reporter got pushy in trying to get a few sound bites or even an interview, but no one would talk. Shortly after, most of the group disbanded and left. The leaders of the group took the cake, signs, and banners to Mora's house where they were staged so he could see them. "Despite not seeing him," said Robinson, "we were told that he heard we were there and was flattered by the gesture. Even though we didn't actually complete the project as intended, we succeeded in letting Mora know that UW wanted him."

Most fans and media types thought the incessant Mora talk was ridiculous. After all, he was under contract with the Seahawks for the 2009 season. If Washington had wanted him, surely they would have hired him the previous December when the opportunity was there. KJR host Ian Furness banned all talk of Mora-to-Washington from his show. "We're only going to discuss realistic candidates," he said. Three years later, when asked if Mora was a candidate, Scott Woodward said: "I'm not going to go into it specifically. But I was going to engage Jim from day one about who he recommended because I knew he wasn't going to be a candidate and had no interest in being a candidate because of his obligation to Vulcan. So I respected that. So it was clear that I wanted to seek his advice and counsel on who we should talk to and where we should go."

But in reality, Emmert and Woodward had offered Mora the Washington job. Inside his Kirkland home, Mora agonized over the dilemma of whether to coach the Seattle Seahawks or the Washington Huskies. At the end of the deliberation process, Mora turned away from his dream job and told Woodward he was remaining with the Seahawks.

For the Huskies, two games remained before the nightmare could be declared over. Pundits nationwide dubbed the upcoming Apple Cup as a matchup of two of the worst teams in college football history. The Washington State Cougars entered the game with a 1-10 record, having only beaten Division II Portland State. The Huskies, of course, were 0-10. Locally, fans referred to it as The Toilet Bowl or The Pillow Fight. As the Huskies got dressed before the game, there was actually a slight uptick to team morale. "The conversation was nothing about Willingham," said Kirton. "We were like 'let's not worry about the younger guys with next year ahead of them. Let's put our differences aside and go out there and play for each other.' Everyone throughout the state cared about the Apple Cup whether they went to those schools or not. To make it worse, we were the two worst teams in America. And we played like it, going double overtime. But for 99% of the game there was a positive vibe."

However, for the Huskies, that last percentage point was pure torture. Washington led 13-10 with thirty-seven seconds left, when Cougar quarterback Kevin Lopina found freshman Jared Karstetter behind a beaten Washington secondary. Karstetter, with only three catches all season, went 48 yards to the Washington 18 yard line. Kicker Nico Grasu drilled a 22-yard field goal to send the game to overtime. In the second OT, Grasu converted a 37-yarder for the 16-13 victory. Martin Stadium erupted as thousands of Cougar fans poured onto the field in screaming celebration. Willingham and his grim-faced players trudged toward the locker room following another crushing defeat. WSU coach Paul Wulff jumped about the field in a comically uncoordinated manner, before giving hugs to his wife and son. Bending forward, he asked the boy a simple question. "Who's still winless?" The boy looked at his dad and beamed a smile, before replying: "The Huskies!"

Washington players were well aware of the winless albatross hanging from their necks. "It was one of the shittiest feelings I've ever had," said fullback Paul Homer. "On the bus ride to the airport I just stared out the window. Then we got on the plane and all I did was stare at the seat in front of me. The Cougars were the worst college team I have ever seen in my life. When I was out on the field, I thought they were worse than our scout team. I couldn't believe that game would be close. I hate talking about that game to be honest with you. I can't understand how our offense couldn't tear that defense apart and score touchdowns at will. And how does Karstetter catch that pass? You know they're going deep. All you have to do is be there and knock the ball away. It's very simple. I was standing right there on the sideline and it happened in front of me. I couldn't believe he caught it."

For Washington, it was now two more agonizing weeks before the season finale against Cal in Berkeley. Several assistant coaches had already cleared out their offices. Boxes were stacked in hallways. Desks were empty. In the most visible manner, the staff was mailing it in.

"Those two weeks before the Cal game seemed like forever," Kirton said. "The words coming out of Willingham's mouth were just air. He was no longer there. My teammates were ready to get these last sixty minutes over with and go home. For myself, I wanted to fight to the end. I wanted at least one win."

But there was no way Washington could win that game. Everyone knew it. Tyrone Willingham's final hours as Washington's football coach proved pitiful. California running back Jahvid Best toyed with Washington, racing for a school record 311 yards rushing and 4 touchdowns in less than three quarters of play. The Bears led 31-0 at halftime and won with ease 48-7. The Washington Huskies were officially the first team in Pac-10 history to go 0-12.

"That game was gut-wrenching," said Kirton. "It hit me that it was really over now. All the effort and time putting in the effort was now a closed book. It was over. I spoke to my family on the field. I spoke to Juan Garcia and Chad Macklin about the things we had gone through.

It was a dead day. That was that. You can fault Willingham for checking out on us. For having no emotion and not preparing for the game. All he seemed prepared for was going back home and moving his family back to wherever."

Seattle-area reporters got confused where to go for post game interviews. They stood on the field, awaiting word, when Bob Condotta of *The Seattle Times* heard his cell phone rang. It was Jeff Bechtold from the UW athletic department, wondering where they were. "Tyrone is up here," he said.

The reporters rushed up a hallway near the locker room. They arrived just in time to glimpse Willingham trying to duck up some stairs. Don Ruiz of *The Tacoma News Tribune* shouted: "Tyrone! Aren't you going to talk to us?" Willingham allowed ninety seconds, exuding an angry defiance as he gave a series of terse responses. Then he terminated the interview, and his tenure at Washington ended as well.

CHAPTER 22

A Visit with Mike Gastineau

Mike Gastineau has been a host for KJR Sports Radio 950 AM since 1991. In September of 1993 he was moved to afternoons, a slot he has anchored ever since. For the past decade, he has co-hosted Washington weekly coach's show during the football season at Anthony's Home Port, alongside the voice of the Huskies, Bob Rondeau.

Derek Johnson: What was it like doing the radio show with Tyrone Willingham?

Mike Gastineau: Amazingly it was really good, especially when it became obvious where everything was heading. Tyrone was always incredibly professional to work with. He never brought a negative attitude to the show. There were times I could tell he was down, and Tyrone was not a dumb man; he knew what was going on and could see what was happening. And we could all argue about what more he could have done to prevent it from happening. While all that was going on, he was never anything less than professional and courteous to me and was a gentleman. He was incredibly easy and positive to work with.

He and I got along. It's a tricky path that you walk on. It's his show, it's called the Tyrone Willingham Show. I'm the host. Later in his career, I think people wanted more of an ambush. But that's not what this show was about. There are plenty of other shows out there for that kind of thing.

You could see everything wearing on him in that last year, there's no doubt about that. But in terms of how he dealt with me and us and regarding the atmosphere of the show, he was a solid pro in the face of some pretty crummy things.

Johnson: When I spoke with athletic director Scott Woodward, he said it was difficult getting to know Tyrone Willingham and getting him to open up.

Gastineau: I understand what Scott is saying. In the context of the show, a lot of the time to talk [personally] was during the three minute commercial breaks during show. Tyrone was not an open person, there's no doubt about that. He was also not a guy who would sit there during the break and complain what was going on or going wrong. He was not a guy I felt like I could buddy up with and joke around with, although he had a better sense of humor than people realized. He was quick with a laugh. There were times where I would wish people would see that side of him. As things got bad he put up this wall around himself.

Johnson: This might be too speculative, but people I've talked to at Notre Dame feel that that situation changed him. You may not be able to judge that if you hadn't spoken with him prior to him coming to Washington.

Gastineau: I talked with Tyrone once or twice when he was the Stanford coach and once as the Notre Dame coach —for phone interviews. You're right, it's speculation. But I think its accurate speculation. I think that the Notre Dame job has the ability to do that to anyone. It takes people in, chews them up and spits them out. He wasn't setting the world on fire there but they weren't horrible either. I mean, Charlie Weis's record the first couple of years there was comparable to Tyrone's. And they extended Charlie but fired Tyrone.

I'm from Indiana, and I know a lot of Notre Dame people back there. When he first got there, there were a lot of positive feelings about him with the winning in the first year. When he started to struggle, my friends started making a point about saying he was the first non-Catholic coach in Notre Dame history. I didn't know what all that meant. I know that they weren't saying that the first year when they were winning games. But in the second and third years they did start saying those things. I can't say for sure if it changed him, but I think the speculation is fair.

Johnson: What was the best moment you can remember occurring during the show?

Gastineau: This sounds obvious, but it was always fun when they won. Because to be honest it didn't happen that often. But it felt like every week we were talking about another loss and it wore us down. But I've done Rick Neuheisel's show, Keith Gilbertson's show, Tyrone Willingham's show and now Steve Sarkisian's show. And what's always fun is that first year. Everyone is happy and excited. There's a possibility that things are going to be great. It was that way when Willingham first got here. In a lot of ways Tyrone Willingham embodied all the things that Washington football stood for. He was an honorable man, he was a no bullshit guy, and he wasn't going to cheat. And based on his record at Stanford and Notre Dame, he was going to win. He certainly wasn't going to be the win-loss disaster he turned out to be.

Johnson: Well speaking personally, I never thought that it was a slam dunk he was going to win. Not at all.

Gastineau: Well not a slam dunk certainly, but it was a pretty good bet. He had won at Stanford and at Notre Dame. He took Stanford to a Rose Bowl, for crying out loud. If you can take Stanford to a Rose Bowl, it stands to reason you can be successful at a place like Washington.

Johnson: Late in the 2007 season there was a civil war of sorts occurring amid the Washington fan base. You came out on the radio on several occasions giving Willingham a staunch defense. What was your perspective at the time?

Gastineau: I come from an old school point of view. I am in favor in letting a coach get four years and fill the roster with his recruits. But Tyrone had two things working against him by that third year. One, the lack of success. Second, the Jim Mora interview when he was with the Atlanta Falcons, where Jim had gone on KJR and said he would drop everything the week of the Super Bowl if he could come back to coach

U-Dub. I think it put an incredible amount of external and internal pressure on Tyrone. Now, of course we can say that that's life in the big leagues and you have to learn to deal with the pressure. But all of sudden the savior was saying "Hey I'll come there whenever you need me." And it allowed the noise, rhetoric and pressure to be cranked to an almost intolerable level. My reasons to defend Tyrone at that point… Well, you would look at the record and be a bit skeptical. But they had injury problems and tough breaks that went against them. I just don't think any college team is going to get better by running guys off every two or three years. Since Don James, they had had Jim Lambright, Rick Neuheisel, Keith Gilbertson and Tyrone Willingham. That was four coaches in [fourteen] years. At some point you've got to stop the carousel and get behind and believe in someone.

Johnson: The belief in Tyrone certainly wavered during that 2008 season. Was there a low point that came while doing the show?

Gastineau: There was a moment in the sixth or seventh week. It was before he was fired but it was clear Tyrone was done. There was a guy who showed up at the coach's show, he was about fifty or fifty five years old. And he was wearing a t-shirt that said HIRE JIM MORA. He stood three feet across from Tyrone and berated him on the air. I remember thinking that it was one of the cruelest things I have ever seen a person do to another person. It was the ultimate example of someone kicking someone else when they were down. You can justify it by saying he was a lousy coach or he's a big dog, but it was a shitty thing to do. Everyone knew what the score was, everyone knew what was going on. It was classless. It was the cruelest thing I have ever seen anybody do. I thought to myself, here's a guy that woke up and said "here's what I am going to do to contribute to the world." What a pathetic thing to do. Tyrone was going to be fired, it was over. His backers were wrong, it was over. And this guy was going to give Tyrone a swift kick to the balls.

Johnson: Did you talk to Tyrone about it?

Gastineau: I talked to him briefly and said "Did you notice the guy's shirt?" Tyrone said yes he had. Then Bob Rondeau said "Why, what happened? Bob hadn't noticed the shirt. But then Bob felt the same way as I did. What a classless thing to do. Especially at a certain age. If you're a college student it's one thing. Maybe when you're twenty you can screw around like that and it's somewhat understandable. But not this guy. He could have asked the question without wearing the shirt. It was beneath the things that the Washington program stands for.

You know, at one point during the 2008 season I asked Tyrone if he wouldn't like to fight back a bit. I told him "Hey, if you want to fight back against a caller, we have your back." Tyrone told me a quick story. Years ago, when he was a graduate assistant at North Carolina State, he was coming off the field at the end of the game. Someone in the stands yelled something racist at him. His reaction was to go after the guy. I don't think any punches were thrown. But when the dust settled and he was back in the locker room, he decided, "I am never going to allow myself to do that again." I think that was a defining moment in his life. I think it shaped his behavior in the years to come.

Johnson: Do you remember any details from the final show in 2008?

Gastineau: During the last show, we all knew it was the last one. It had been incredibly uncomfortable. That last year was pure hell for everybody. I will reiterate, Tyrone is an intelligent man. He knew it was failing, he knew he was failing, and he knew it was the most public of all failures. And it was a brutal thing to watch someone go through.

The win-loss ratio was irritating to everybody, but he had always been a gentleman to everyone. He was so good to everyone. And everyone at Anthony's was very sad. I know there was probably a lot of joy in the fan base to see him leave town, but there wasn't any joy for people who knew him through the coach's show. People were sad. It was a shame to see. I hate to see a person publicly fail that way. That last night we shook hands and the people at Anthony's cooked dinner for him to take home to his wife. They had also bought flowers for his wife in the hopes she would come, but she wasn't coming to any of the shows. The whole thing was just sad.

Soon-to-be athletic director Scott Woodward was privately ambivalent about President Emmert's decision to bring Willingham back for the 2008 season.

CHAPTER 23

Woodward Reflects

"Willingham will stay on for the remaining five games this season before leaving with a $1 million buyout, UW athletic director Scott Woodward announced Monday."

—*Tacoma News Tribune,* October 2008

IT was while Todd Turner was still athletic director at Washington that Scott Woodward decided he wanted to take over the job. In the middle of a game at Husky Stadium when miserable weather moved in and Washington's performance verged toward macabre, he found himself impressed by the resolute fan base. "I remember looking into the stands while it was raining and they're hanging in there," Woodward said. "It was during the 2007 season that I said 'I want this job.' If they're coming out for this bad of product, what will they do when we're winning? They will come back in droves. The U-Dub's rightful place is in the top three in the Pac-10. That's what we're building back toward. I see it long term, building with foundations."

When President Emmert fired Todd Turner in December 2007, he gave the interim position to Woodward to manage while searching for a replacement. Come September 2008, Emmert concluded the search by removing the interim tag from Woodward and making it permanent.

Scott Woodward grew up in Baton Rouge, Louisiana. As a young kid, his athletic specialty wasn't football, but tennis. As a teenager, he studied at the knee of political strategist James Carville, who went on to become the future adviser to Bill Clinton on campaigns for U.S. Senate and governor's races in the South.

Following his graduation from Louisiana State University, Woodward started his own public relations firm. While there, he formed strong ties with Louisiana State Chancellor Mark Emmert, who soon after tabbed Woodward to become director of external affairs for his alma mater. Woodward ultimately followed Emmert to Washington to fulfill the same role, before taking over for the fired Todd Turner in early 2008.

As the vast majority of Husky players struggled emotionally with the news of Willingham's retention, they slogged through winter conditioning drills in the Dempsey Indoor—as Tyrone and his ever-present golf club oversaw the action. Woodward harbored concerns about Willingham as a coach, but felt great respect for him as a person.

"I was very impressed with who he is, because Tyrone is a good man and a great father obviously and husband," Woodward said. "You can't help but see that he exudes goodness. That was what I liked about him and what I was impressed with. But he never let that veneer down. That's who he is. I think I understand Tyrone better than a lot of people do. He's an African-American from the South, and I have very many African American friends from the south. I hate to generalize, but he comes from a military family. They're stern and strict and there are a lot of things that are interesting in growing up that way. So I understood where he was coming from."

Having come from LSU, Woodward had been a rabid football fan of the Tigers, and witnessed their 2003 National Championship season. He attended many practices and saw legendary coach Nick Saban up close and personal.

"Nick was very involved in the teaching and active participation in practice," Woodward said. "And Tyrone was more of an overseer. Nick would go from drill to drill. He would coach the defensive backs like he was the position coach. He was very similar –not in personality but in management style—with Steve Sarkisian. Sark is very intimately involved with the quarterbacks and offense. Nick is very involved with the d-backs and defense. And I like that. Because to me, to have success you need to do two things very well. Understand the game, and love to recruit. And these two guys love those things. And I don't think Tyrone liked to recruit. I live by the mantra that it's not the Xs and Os but the Jimmys and Joes. I tell Sark that all the time: Using the bad clichés makes the good coaches great and average coaches good. And then you need to have the knowledge and special something about the game, the ability to teach it and execute it to be great. And that's what I saw in Steve Sarkisian. For my style, Tyrone was more of a coach that liked to oversee and delegate. That works for some people. It worked for Don James, even though he understood the game very well."

Despite Woodward's attempts to involve himself in the football program, Willingham endeavored to keep him at arm's length. The coach was a hard guy to get to know and he kept a constant barrier up. Their relationship was cordial, but as more time went by, most of Woodward's communication was with members of the coaching staff as opposed to directly with Willingham.

When it came to Willingham's handling of the media, Woodward winced at seeing his coach's rudeness and paranoia. Woodward put on a unified front for the sake of public relations. "I was sympathetic to those guys [in the Seattle media] but never showed it. I backed [Tyrone] 100% on his access. I thought at times his media skills lacked, not because he didn't know how but because he didn't want to. He viewed the media as the enemy."

Speaking of enemies, there was none greater than Oregon, as the Huskies opened their 2008 season in Eugene. Sitting in the guest suite at Autzen Stadium, Woodward looked on as the Ducks dismantled the Huskies 44-10. He unleashed a torrent of profanity as he saw the season's writing on the wall. "Psychologically, I had grave concerns after that Oregon game," he said. "It was a disappointment. I thought we would be better prepared. We were totally outmanned and totally unprepared. I knew in my gut then that it was not going to be a good season. Overall, I just saw that we were getting our butts kicked in the fourth quarter. That's a team of poor conditioning and poor preparation. I saw that it was one of the key factors. You know the rest of the story, the kids especially in the interior were overweight and slow, and fast teams like Oregon kicked their butt."

Five more games went by, all of them losses. By the season's halfway point, Washington was 0-6 and attendance was paltry as the fans stayed away in droves. Public pressure proved almost unbearable as fans clamored for a mid-season firing. With the Notre Dame Fighting Irish coming to town, Woodward had decisions to make.

"The Notre Dame game was telling," Woodward said. "I knew we were going to make a change and I wanted to get an early start on the process of looking for our next coach. Tyrone and I began discussions on how we were going to exit the stage. He was very disappointed. He was extremely upset about it. He took it hard, like competitors do. They were not fun conversations.

"I had made the decision, right or wrong, that the head coach should remain in place," Woodward said. "I had been in places where I had seen bad behavior and off-the-field problems became highly probable. And so I used the term of not wanting an orphaned team. I thought that with the [remaining] games having a leader in place was the right way to go. I thought it was going to create some relief and they could go out and play, with pressure taken off and go out and have fun, But they quit, essentially."

Following the 2008 Apple Cup – another Husky collapse—the team was now 0-11. On his way out of Pullman and to the airport, Woodward pulled over where no one else was around and screamed into a field. He would later describe that day as being the all-time low for himself. That Washington could lose to a horrible Cougar team was unacceptable. But there was no going back—for the outcome was permanently in the books. Woodward struggled privately with self-doubt.

"I knew we had to move on and I felt bad for the kids because the experience was so bad," Woodward said. "If I had to do it again, I might have picked an interim coach and done it right there. But that was my thing at the time. Making sure the kids are doing what they're supposed to do in the classroom and off the field and we will fix the competitive problem by thinking about the hiring process."

"Tyrone was always a gentleman and always exuded integrity. I never saw him waver from that, but as far as individual players I heard some things. I was triaging and focusing on getting a new coach."

When asked about Jim L. Mora, Woodward was quick to state he never met with him while conducting the coaching search. When pressed, he said that he spoke with Mora many times on the phone in seeking counsel. But in reality, Emmert and Woodward envisioned a fiery and charismatic new coach leading the Huskies in the future. That led them to offer Mora the Washington job. After agonizing over the decision, Mora turned down the offer to remain with the Seahawks. Woodward and Emmert went on to meet with Steve Sarkisian on Thanksgiving evening and saw those same desirable qualities in him. Soon after, Sarkisian was hired as the next UW coach.

When asked to sum up Willingham's time at Washington, Woodward was succinct. "Tyrone Willingham was a good man," he said. "But he was a bad fit at the University of Washington. The wrong man at the wrong time."

Washington's new coach Steve Sarkisian instructs quarterback Jake Locker

CHAPTER 24

Sark Comes to Washington

"I share the same expectations as the Husky fan base and I fully expect that we will return Washington to the top of the Pac-10 Conference and compete for national championships."

—UW football coach Steve Sarkisian, December 2008

IN the final days of Washington's horrific 0-12 season, Husky players were weary of where the next punch was coming from. The pulse-quickening rumors about Jim L. Mora had fizzled to naught. Then word leaked from ESPN that USC's offensive coordinator Steve Sarkisian badly wanted the job. He had friends in the coaching profession lobbying Scott Woodward and President Emmert to select him.

At first, Woodward gave no comment and speculation percolated for a few days. But soon, he announced that Sarkisian was indeed the next Washington coach. He and Emmert had been blown away by Sarkisian's interview and believed his youthful energy to be the perfect elixir for a listless team.

"We were surprised that a USC coach would be considered," recalled fullback Paul Homer. "It seemed weird, but I was also excited since they had been so successful. When I watched his first press conference, he seemed a little goofy. I thought to myself: What are we doing?

"But in first team meeting he laid down the law and said we're no longer playing like garbage," Homer said. "He was full of positive energy and excitement. He said if we didn't do what the coaching staff says we would be gone. That gave me the biggest smile of my life. It was a new positive energy that made me the most happy. They said if we buy in they would take us to the very top. That got everybody fired up."

In one of the first meetings in the team room, Sarkisian stood before the team and said: "There's somebody here that would like to talk to you guys." Suddenly, legendary UW quarterback Marques Tuiasosopo entered the room. The players hooted and hollered. Tuiasosopo told of his time being coached by Sarkisian while with the Oakland Raiders, where Sarkisian was an assistant. Then Tuiasosopo held up his fist and showed off his 2001 Rose Bowl Championship ring. "If you guys work hard and believe in Sark, you can have one of these." The players jumped to their feet in excitement.

Tuiasosopo then rocked the room back on its heels, as he launched into the "Say Who?" chant.

"When he first started it, we looked at each other like: is this okay for us to do?" said Homer. "And then everybody started shouting the Say Who chant. We were in a frenzy. It was freaking awesome."

W

91
32

CHAPTER 25

A Visit with "Angry Alum"

In the fall of 2007, while tense public debate raged throughout western Washington over whether to retain Tyrone Willingham, one of the battlefields became the message boards at Dawgman.com. One of the most erudite voices belonged to a poster going by the screen name "Angry Alum", also known as Larry. As a graduate of the University of Washington and diehard Husky football fan, Angry Alum publicly expressed his concerns over Willingham's job performance and the strange manner in which the media and many fans were defending the coach to the bitter end.

Derek Johnson: When did you first have grave concerns that Willingham was not the right man to lead the Washington Huskies?

Angry Alum: I was immediately underwhelmed at the hire because of his previous record, but eventually resigned myself into a 'he's here now, let's see what he can do' mentality. I did want very badly to see a black coach succeed at Washington, and like many fans, came around and rooted hard for Tyrone as soon as the ball was in the air.

The 2-9 record in 2005 was easy to write off as the residue of a 1-10 team. 2006 had an extremely promising start, and then the team fizzled late with some injuries. That happens every year to somebody, and wasn't yet a valid reason to throw Tyrone to the wolves. But I started to see his tenure as an irredeemable failure after the loss to Stanford. Losing at home to an 0-10 team when the Huskies had entered the game on track for bowl eligibility was the unmistakable moment when the wheels came off. That game convinced me that Coach Willingham wouldn't succeed here.

Johnson: The popular refrain among fans and media was that Willingham was brought in to clean up the program. What is your take on that?

Angry Alum: It was overwrought. Even service academies have football players get into trouble. If a 24/7 regimented and militarized existence can't keep athletes on the straight and narrow, why would we expect a single person's influence to? A kid at an academy has constant daily access to hundreds of extraordinarily disciplined and high caliber people for four years from dawn to dark. From Annapolis alone in recent years, there have been failed drug tests, academic fraud, and rape arrests tied to the football program. One guy got two years for sexual assault. If guys can manage to get in trouble there, they'll get in trouble anywhere, regardless of whether or not the coach is of high character.

Even if you play devil's advocate and grant the point that the program was an outlier and needed to be reeled in, Coach Willingham had never been in a position of needing to do that before at Stanford or Notre Dame. There was zero track record. There have been many business books written about the type of leadership needed to transform an organization culturally, and there's a hell of a lot more to it than just being a principled individual, which is precisely what many people were hanging their hats on when explaining why Willingham would change the culture here. I still think the logic behind that was pretty flimsy.

Johnson: In the final weeks of the 2007 season, a civil war broke out amongst Husky fans. Washington had solidified a third straight losing under Willingham and fans that wanted him fired had seen enough. Those defending Willingham were doing so with a fierce defiance. People like Shaun Alexander of the Seahawks and groups like the NAACP sounded their support for Willingham. What did you see happening around you?

Angry Alum: It was more personal than I'd ever seen it. Some people I talked to on both sides were extremely visceral in their positions. I had a guy throw a punch at me over it. Washington had just fired Keith Gilbertson three years beforehand, and it never even approached that level. People seemed to universally agree that he needed to go. There was definitely something different about this situation.

One of the things that irritated me was that many of the people who insisted that Coach Willingham stay did not (or if they did, we never heard about it) insist that he be considered for openings at their own programs.

Johnson: What did those intense weeks tell you about society in general and about Seattle fans?

Angry Alum: I interpreted the desire to keep him here despite poor performance as an attempt to turn the Washington football program into a social experiment. Sometimes, people would tell me outright, 'we've got to give a black man a chance to succeed here'. Bear in mind, this was after having gone 11-25 in the previous three years. He'd already been given a chance to succeed, and had failed in spectacular fashion.

My perception of that was that there definitely was a vocal subset of the fanbase that wanted Tyrone to succeed because it seemed 'right' and would be a high profile validation for some dearly held beliefs. I also wanted Tyrone to succeed, in part for the very same reasons. I shared (and still share) their convictions. I believe very strongly, in big red bold letters, that there are not enough black coaches in the college game, and that needs to change. The difference is that when it became clear that he wasn't going to be a success, some people couldn't divorce the two. Coach Willingham failing was not in any sense a proxy failure for all black coaches everywhere.

You can't just generalize one guy and try to apply it across a range of other people. That's what was distasteful about it to me. These guys are individuals, let's judge them as individuals based on their performance and merit. That's the fair thing to do. Whether Tyrone was a wild success or a dismal failure, it doesn't mean other black coaches will be the same. Looking at things in this way enabled me to be comfortable in concluding that he wasn't a good fit for Washington, and not feel like I was trading away anything I believed in.

Johnson: On December 5, 2007, President Emmert announced that Tyrone Willingham was being brought back for a fourth year. What was your reaction?

Angry Alum: The 'is he gone or not?' chatter was non-stop after Washington blew a 21-0 first quarter lead to lose the Hawaii game. Everyone I talked to was convinced he'd be fired. We were hearing rumors saying it was all but a done deal, that it had already happened in Hawaii, but had not yet been announced. Another rumor was that Jim L. Mora had already signed a contract to take over the team. So I skipped in to work on Wednesday expecting to hear that Willingham would be gone. We finally heard the awful news that he would be returning, and I felt like I had been kicked in the stomach. Like many people, I've had things go wrong in the workplace at some of the earlier stops in my career. I've worked for one or two genuinely malignant assholes. I've been yelled at. I've lost jobs. I got laid off on Christmas Eve once. No matter what, you always maintain that stiff upper lip at work. Emotion is for some other time and place. You want to cry in your beer, you do it at home. Work is for work. Not on December 5, 2007.

Tyrone was staying. I knew 2008 was dead. I just sat down and buried my head in my hands, and then these hot, angry tears came out of my face, and I had to leave immediately. I was breaking a cardinal rule and losing control at work, but I couldn't have helped it - Washington didn't give a shit about football anymore.

Johnson: Do you feel the media influenced Emmert's decision to bring Willingham back the fourth year?

Angry Alum: I have no idea. Sometimes I think he did exactly what he wanted to do. I don't buy the excuse that his hands were tied. Beyond that, I gave up trying to deconstruct any thought process that would have led anyone to the conclusion that an 11-25 coach should have been retained. Just can't get my head around it.

In any case, I think he should have personally absorbed more of the responsibility for 0-12. Keeping Tyrone Willingham for the fourth year, in defiance of the facts, was solely an executive decision, and very arguably one of the worst in the history of sports. Dr. Emmert owns that.

Johnson: During both the 2007 and 2008 seasons you went to Anthony's Home Port during the Tyrone Willingham radio show and took the microphone to address the coach. What happened?

Angry Alum: I should point out that Coach Willingham, to his personal credit, was unfailingly cordial and professional in my discussions with him. He was never rude to me, even though I made absolutely no efforts to hide the fact that I thought he should be removed.

It started right after the string of losses in 2007 that prompted Coach Willingham and Dr. Turner to blame the players almost exclusively for the team's lack of success. I was equally bothered both by what I saw as very limited objection in the Seattle media and the actual comments. So I went to the show to ask him why he'd chosen to fault the players, but not assign any blame to the coaching staff. I remember telling him that I thought his actions marked a serious failure as an educator of young people. That was the deeper offense to me, and I just wanted to look him in the eye and tell him that.

I talked to him again, after the Oregon game in 2008, which I was in Eugene for, because I was just dumbfounded that he'd gotten a reprieve from getting fired and nine months later, the team still looked disorganized and unprepared. I did tell him that I thought we'd be lucky to win two games.

Johnson: Your dad disapproved of your stance. What were those conversations with him like?

Angry Alum: My dad was disappointed that I'd gone after another black man in a public way. We were never tense or upset about it, just disagreed. I love, respect, and admire my dad, but we're products of different times and places, and just saw things completely differently. He grew up in the inner city during the middle of the civil rights movement. I grew up 25 years later under considerably better circumstances, thanks entirely to my folks' hard work. So my dad was born in 1955, the year Rosa Parks told a bus driver to pound sand. The guy was almost a teenager before he could take a leak without being reminded by the government of his own country that they thought he was inferior.

Having that kind of strife as the backbeat of your formative years absolutely has to shape and inform the way that you see issues like the ones we faced with Ty Willingham. There is no way around it. So our differences of opinion are not because I'm smarter or more worldly than my dad (I'm absolutely not), but because we just had such tremendously different backgrounds.

My opinion was that if you wanted to see more black coaches in college football (and we both did), the worst thing you could do was treat a high profile guy with kid gloves. You treat him the same as any other coach - set high expectations, and then judge his performance objectively based on results. If he loses, fire his ass, just like anybody else. If he wins, bar the doors so he can't leave. But it should be 100% performance based. It's counterintuitive, but I see that as the clearest path to enabling more high level hires of black coaches.

Trying to remove performance from the equation in a performance driven job just doesn't make sense. It's football, and we have a scoreboard. Many jobs have much more subjective success criteria - it's not like a sous chef or a TV anchor or a librarian has a W-L record. But a football coach does, and we should use it.

Johnson: Many fans excitedly anticipated the 2008 season. Were you caught up in the optimism?

Angry Alum: No, I had given up in 2006 after the Stanford game. I considered both 2007 and 2008 a waste before the opening kickoff. I felt awful for the players going into 2008 more than anything.

Johnson: Do you think the Willingham situation at Washington hampered the hopes for more black head coaches to be given opportunities at Division I football programs in the future?

Angry Alum: Without a doubt, and I don't think there's anything earth shattering about that. It's based on something not exclusive to college football, race, or Tyrone Willingham: Risk aversion. It's human nature. Nobody wants to hire someone who's going to be messy to fire.

That's why Western Europe usually has a much higher

unemployment rate than the United States, and why many people won't hire relatives, it's also why companies do background checks for even routine hires, and I suspect that's at least part of the reason why Mike Leach is having a hard time finding another job.

Somewhere, maybe at an FCS or lower division school, there's a young black position coach plugging away in obscurity hoping against the odds to work his way up the ranks. High profile, racially tinged situations like the one we had render guys trying to get in the door a powerful disservice. They are infinitely better off if their potential future employers know that they can evaluate their performance, good or bad, without race being called into question one way or the other.

It will mark great progress when some of the stakeholders who share in the opinion that the low number of black coaches is a blight on the sport are willing to push for the removal of a black coach who is clearly failing. It'll certainly lead to more open and productive public discussions on the topic.

Johnson: Looking back on the Willingham era at Washington, how does your mind reconcile those four years?

Angry Alum: Besides my own warm bed, Husky Stadium on game day is my favorite place on earth. I get to be there six times a year, for four hours at a time. That's just 24 hours a year, or one day a year, and four years were made worthless. I'll never get that back, and neither will anybody else. It may sound strange, but having to watch the team go 11-37 over those four years caused me a lot of heartache and anguish. There was a very real sense of loss. I'm glad it's behind us, but we could've saved a lot of frustration had we all just been clear-headed and plainspoken about the fact that he was failing.

Ironically, those who struggled to keep Coach Willingham in place in spite of his performance did him no favors. Keeping him in a job that wasn't going well never improved the situation, and ultimately led to 0-12, which probably ended his career. Tyrone Willingham himself was probably ill-served by some of his strongest supporters.

Epilogue

"A nation or civilization that continues to produce soft-minded men purchases its own spiritual death on the installment plan."

—Martin Luther King, Jr.

IN the wake of his firing at Washington, Tyrone Willingham granted an interview with Fred Mitchell of *The Chicago Tribune.* Mitchell steered the topic toward the plight of black head coaches in college football. Fresh off Washington's 0-12 season, Willingham revealed his inner thoughts.

"It has always been the downtrodden [programs] that we've had to take over," Willingham said. "There are a lot of things not right with those situations. The degree of difficulty is enhanced in those programs. You do the best you can with the resources around you. I have always tried to keep the personal part out of it, keep it, for the most part, strictly professional, because there are labels and stereotypes: [Blacks] are more physical and not analytical, that we're more emotional than analytical. We've had a lot of things to deal with over the years, and I'm hopeful that some of those things are being erased as we speak, so that my son will not have to deal with this."

To many embittered fans back in Seattle, the comments were a slap in the face. In looking back to December 2004, when Willingham became the Husky coach, Washington had had only one losing season in the past twenty-seven years. In that time, the Huskies had been to seven Rose Bowls, an Orange Bowl, and won a national championship. Keith Gilbertson's 2004 recruiting class was ranked 19th in the nation by Rivals.com. The program's graduation rate from the previous year was 67%, which was second in the Pac-10 only to Stanford.

Nobody argued against the dismissal of UW coach Keith Gilbertson after just two seasons. Everyone knew he needed to go after the 1-10 debacle. He was also white, so when Turner fired him there was no mess, no muss. When Willingham took over, he inherited a group of players craving encouragement and competent direction. As Willingham began molding Husky football to fit his vision, he was doing so in one of the softest, most self-congratulating liberal regions in America. After his first couple losing seasons, standards for Husky football were lowered to accommodate his failings. To a large section of the fan base, it no longer mattered whether Willingham fielded winning teams or struggled. The "air of the program" became the priority as opposed to results. People swelled with pride at seeing the first black head coach patrolling UW's sideline and they projected onto him whatever qualities they wished him to have. Problem was, he wasn't the person people thought him to be. He looked disciplined, but his players were often out of position. He came across as tough, but his teams were mentally weak. He projected confidence, but his teams were crippled with self-doubt. He seemed well-spoken and wise, but often talked in circles and left players bewildered. As losses piled up and playing careers were cratered, the self-congratulating liberals of Seattle cheered him on, sometimes in rousing, defiant fashion. Willingham's likeness appeared everywhere, including on a giant poster plastered to the side of Husky Stadium. But by the time the Huskies were the nation's laughingstock with leaked stories of Willingham's petulant behavior, the damage had been done—damage that was preventable.

A month later in January 2009, two million Americans—young and old, rich and poor, black and white, assembled in Washington DC, crowding the gleaming white Capitol Building and extending all the way to the Washington Monument and Lincoln Memorial in the distance. They unleashed thunderous roars of approval for Barack Obama as he was inaugurated as the nation's 44th president. Millions more across the country watched on TV and celebrated. School kids in countless classrooms witnessed the nation's first African-American president address the crowd while flanked by red, white and blue balloons.

When Obama assumed the presidency of the United States, he inherited an economy that was sinking into recession and in need of a shot in the arm. He stepped into the spotlight of a left-dominated media that was thrilled by his arrival. Many Americans on both sides of the political aisle were pleased to see the departure of his presidential predecessor George W. Bush.

But when Obama first took over, he immediately began breaking campaign promises and enacting a radical agenda. Backed by a breathless media, Obama could do no wrong in the eyes of the mainstream. His suave message inspired millions to imagine he was spearheading a warm, caring government that would ease people's struggles and give them a better life. Problem was, the rhetoric distracted the nation from what was really happening. Obama claimed he needed $871 billion for a Stimulus Package to keep the nation's unemployment rate from topping 8%, but within two years it reached 10%. He repeatedly assured Americans that he'd protect Medicare against cuts, but then pressed for the passage of bills that include savage cuts in Medicare. He criticized George Bush's deficit spending and promised to halt that practice if elected, but two years into his presidency he'd quadrupled the size of the deficit to almost $2 trillion. He had promised that he wouldn't sign a healthcare bill that would add one dime to the federal deficit, but the bill that Congress rammed through in 2010 added trillions in new federal spending. Even as the deficit ballooned and campaign pledges evaporated, self-congratulating liberals cheered him on, and angrily denounced those who dared to criticize. Obama's likeness appeared everywhere, especially on posters and bumper stickers in stylized stencil portrait, with "progress", "hope", or "change" below his image. By the time many Americans awakened to what was really happening, great damage had been inflicted upon the economy.

The twin tales of Willingham and Obama tell Americans something about themselves. The occurrence of a university's first black coach and a nation's first black leader could have been special moments of legitimate celebration. And yet two men—arguably incompetent and disingenuous—attained powerful roles they had no business assuming. In each case, the projection of white guilt onto these men provided a catalyst to their careers. Generations of white Americans, bearing no actual responsibility for the sins of slavery past, are indoctrinated into shouldering the heavy blame of their ancestors. In their haste to overcompensate, white liberals worshipped at the altars of Obama and Willingham.

The Willingham and Obama stories could have been beautiful if handled differently. Truly competent and honorable men could have become the nation's first black president and Washington's first black head football coach. Their success would help disprove the myths of racial inferiority that made affirmative action deemed necessary. But that didn't happen. Instead, toxic scenarios continued to play out in a society plagued by white guilt where certain blacks adopt a sense of self-righteous entitlement. American society needs to mature in order to realize Martin Luther King, Jr.'s vision of a world where "...people will not be judged by the color of their skin, but by the content of their character."

Less than three months into Obama's presidency, he was largely judged by the color of his skin when he won the 2009 Nobel Peace Prize. His supporters cheered the achievement wildly while others scratched their heads at the unmerited absurdity. As time went by, the soaring rhetoric and bold promises that won Obama the presidency began to create a chasm between fluffy feel-good speeches and hard reality. As citizens gradually realized what was happening it was still too late: Obama's radical Marxist agenda had dealt a devastating blow to America's economic strength and standing in the world.

In the final analysis, Tyrone Willingham fares no better. Here was someone feeling indignant over the public spectacle of his Notre Dame firing—and further shamed by taking a job at "downtrodden" Washington. In truth, he was earning $1.5 million a year, while quietly banking an additional $650,000 every year from Notre Dame between 2005-2009 as part of his severance package. Winning percentage notwithstanding, Willingham possessed immense pride. Whatever history said about his position as a black man, he was going to determine the terms by which he'd be taken. But as he saw, an enormous price was to be paid for harboring an indignant pride. The very thing that allowed him to save face from his Notre Dame firing was a precursor to the epic damage to come at Washington. When he encountered Seattle's community of self-congratulating liberals, the pitiful powder keg was in place that ultimately blew the entire Husky football program to smithereens.

One player whose Husky career died on the vine was running back J.R. Hasty. Whether the blame lies mostly with him or Willingham is conjecture; Hasty smoked pot and periodically jeopardized his academic eligibility. Nonetheless, teammates believed him to be a high quality running back. But Willingham sent Hasty straight into the doghouse, never to return. While there, Hasty watched many fans and media fawn over Willingham as being a great man of integrity and dignity.

"I just thought it was bullshit," Hasty said. "The media didn't know, they just looked at this black guy who is speaking with such intelligence and smooth with his words, and he used his words to shield what was really going on. He would talk in circles and go around the subject and act like he was deep in details. But there were no details; that was bullshit. There were no details or structure. It was all B.S.

"A lot of people didn't want to say it. At the time he was almost the only black head coach in America. So he went for the image. He went for the image of wanting to look like a super sophisticated guy because he was a man of color. He felt he couldn't mess up because he feared they would get rid of him as fast as the next guy, so he stuck to that script. He had come from the South. When he finally got the chance to become a head coach, he was 'I have a college degree, you have to respect me now. I'm the head coach of a major university, I don't have to do much. I will let my assistant coaches do all the work. Why do I need to do anything more, haven't I done enough? I'm going to talk to boosters and use big words and act like I'm an educated man to be respected. I'm going to walk around and act like I'm a victim of color.' And yet the only color that matters is the purple on your jersey. The only number that matters is the number of wins on the left side of the ledger. That was the wrong mindset to have. Because in your last year at Washington, you went 0-12."

Acknowledgements

I would like to thank the following people for their valuable input or support: The several dozen Husky players and various people close to the program who spoke on and off the record; Herb Mead, Tod Jones, Dawn Cahoon, Tom Lemming, Hugh Millen, Mike Gastineau, Mark Emmert, Scott Woodward, Bob Condotta, Jamal and Staci Fountaine, TraeAnna Holiday, Jane Sheppard, Kim Grinolds, Larry the Angry Alum, Scott Farrar, Scott Liljedahl, Jason Pingree, Ron and Margaret Johnson, Jennifer Johnson and the lovely and talented Michelle Sanayebakhsherad for her "creative" title suggestions.